JOURNAL OF DEVELOPING AREAS
Western Illinois University
Macomb, Illinois   61455

Prof.
Marvin Alisky
ASU
Political Science

PSYCHOLOGICAL CHALLENGES TO MODERNIZATION

Psychological Challenges to Modernization

Albert Lauterbach

 Elsevier Scientific Publishing Company
Amsterdam · London · New York 1974

ELSEVIER SCIENTIFIC PUBLISHING COMPANY
335 JAN VAN GALENSTRAAT
P.O. BOX 211, AMSTERDAM, THE NETHERLANDS

AMERICAN ELSEVIER PUBLISHING COMPANY
52 VANDERBILT AVENUE
NEW YORK, NEW YORK 10017, U.S.A.

Library of Congress Card Number: 73-83397

ISBN 0-444-41148-8

Printed in The Netherlands

Acknowledgements

Earlier versions of some chapters have been published in various places. In all these cases the form has been substantially revised and many editorial changes, cuts and additions have been made. Other parts of the book are printed here for the first time.

For the opportunity to use materials published earlier in their original form, I am much obliged to *Kyklos*, Basle; *The American Journal of Psychotherapy*, New York; the Social Science Research Council, New York; Grune and Stratton, Inc., New York; and *The Sarah Lawrence Journal*, Bronxville, New York.

My sincere thanks go to Dr. Joseph Wilder for his collaboration in chapter 6 and his stimulating suggestions in the course of many years.

Contents

Introduction

The common thread in this book is the interpretation of the quest for "progress," especially the modernization trends in various parts of the world, as an array of specific processes in the human mind, rather than as impersonal advances in technological or managerial organization. This psychological view of social change applies, in somewhat different ways, both to those nations which the prevailing terminology classifies as developed and to those which are usually called underdeveloped, newly developing, or modernizing. The semantic and conceptual differences involved will be discussed presently.

In one way or another all the parts of this volume are concerned with psychological interpretations of modernization, either in a general way or in their specific applications to international affairs, development planning, enterprise management, social reform movements, and the social bases of mental health. In a broad sense, this volume continues the explorations attempted in my earlier books *Man, Motives, and Money: Psychological Frontiers of Economics*, and *Enterprise in Latin America: Business Attitudes in a Developing Economy.*

The terminology used throughout this book cannot entirely escape the semantic pitfalls imposed by the loose and constantly changing use of various terms in the still growing literature on "development." An attempt is made, however, to minimize confusion by using the pertinent terms, as consistently as possible, in the following way (this will be clarified more elaborately in the final two chapters):

Modernization, which has been chosen to serve here as the key concept, refers to bringing the technology, economic and social institutions and policies, administrative processes, and attitudinal framework of an indigent nation or major population group up to date in reference to its own felt or latent needs and aspirations, not necessarily those of wealthier, more "developed" nations. A great variety of implementing methods and procedures for modernization is to be expected. Modernization in this sense, we repeat, may or may not coincide with Western or, for that matter, Soviet-type Eastern experiences from the past or present, and is not confined to technological or organizational changes. When we speak here of modernization we mean, as a rule, processes of fairly recent date which are likely to continue for a long time.

Transformation will be occasionally mentioned in both a broader and a narrower sense than modernization. Transformation is a broader concept insofar as it may include some changes that are peripheral if not irrelevant to the fundamental, revolutionary aspects of modernization, and it is narrower to the degree that it may confine itself to specific kinds of felt needs and aspirations, for example, those for a better industrial technology or administrative structure.

The term *change* is used to denote a variety of economic and social adjustments, spontaneous or not, either in the highly industrialized or in the modernizing countries, for example, new approaches to taxation or public housing.

Growth refers to the expansion of economic activities within the existing framework of society, especially ownership and power structure. It applies chiefly to industrialized countries with elaborate and relatively stable institutions.

Development, only yesterday the most widely used term in describing recent happenings in, or strivings of, poverty-stricken populations, has become an almost unusable concept. It has been found that this concept tends to obscure, rather than illuminate, the nature of these processes: it usually confines them to an expected imitation of Western experiences and interprets them as an economic procedure, disregarding their cultural, psychological, and political aspects. In this book, therefore, development concepts will only be used in reference to the terminology employed by others or to derivative and widely accepted meanings, such as development planning.

The first chapter discusses the essence of the socio-economic aspirations of the modernizing nations, the roots and manifestations of totalitarian mentality and behavior, and the reasons for the special attraction of totalitarian "solutions" to these nations.

The second chapter deals with the effects of the modernization process on the rise and the forms of movements for social reform in modernizing areas. This includes the connection between social protest and the search for national identity, distinctions between the various social classes and leadership groups that may spearhead such movements, and the difference between the "Western" labor movements and the social reform groupings in modernizing areas.

The third chapter concentrates on that former model for modernizing nations, the United States, especially the psycho-cultural roots of its international behavior. An attempt is made to trace the reasons for the difficulty encountered by many Americans in understanding either the outside world or their own society, a difficulty resulting largely from their childhood upbringing. The attitudes and missionary self-images thus created, along with various intrinsic contradictions, help explain United States' behavior toward the rest of the world, including the modernizing nations.

The fourth chapter offers a view of the contemporary atmosphere of uncertainty and rapid change of environment, in which the Western business world operates. It thus shows implicitly that modernization as such cannot be expected to remove all the socio-psychological problems that are connected with business activity.

The fifth chapter applies these considerations to the situation facing businessmen and enterprise managers in modernizing countries, and to the role of managerial and entrepreneurial attitudes within the process of modernization.

The sixth chapter, written in collaboration with the psychiatrist Joseph Wilder, M.D., is concerned with the relationship between the existing socio-economic structure and processes of change on the one hand, and the concept and state of mental health in "developed" societies on the other. It also discusses possible applications of these experiences to new kinds of emotional needs that emerge in modernizing populations.

The seventh chapter applies the preceding thoughts to a more general re-examination of the concepts of development and modernization, especially in regard to their application to the changing attitudinal framework in both the industrialized and the modernizing countries. It then raises the related question of to what extent various forms of the modernization process have been conceptually displacing the more conventional typologies of "economic systems."

The final chapter discusses the present disappointment of both the aid-giving and the recipient nations with the development idea, especially with the results of foreign development aid and the imitative and technological approaches to development. It then deals with some recent re-interpretations of what development is.

The book is designed to stimulate continued reconsideration of the attitudinal changes brought about, or required, by the striving toward modernization of many nations in our time — changes involving not only these nations but also the wealthier societies of East and West.

CHAPTER 1

The Modernizing Nations and the Totalitarian Lure

Juan Gonzáles is a South American Indian who lives in a tribal village high in the Andes mountains. He cannot read or write in any language and cannot even speak Spanish, the official language of "his" country. On no day in his life has he eaten the amount of calories, vitamins, or proteins that North American and European experts prescribe as the minimum required in order to keep body and soul together.

His religion is a strange mixture of Christian and pagan elements. He has probably heard of Jesus but certainly not of either Adam Smith or Karl Marx. His most persistent and, as a rule, all-pervading concern is how to grow enough food for himself and his family in order to survive. If possible, he would also like to keep his shack from going to pieces and to have the women weave him a new mat and poncho before the old ones fall apart. North American worries on how to spend one's time and money sensibly in The Affluent Society certainly are not Juan's worries, and will not be those of his sons or grandsons.

He has never heard of free enterprise, or of nationalization of the means of production, nor of liberalism, conservatism, socialism, or any other-ism, though he may have experienced some locally diluted version of *personalismo*, the official glorification of some general or other who happens to be the national dictator of the moment in a distant capital city which Juan can never hope to see.

1

Perceptions of Poverty and Wealth of Nations

For hundreds of millions of people in Latin America, Asia and Africa such concepts as capitalism and socialism remain completely meaningless in reference to their daily life experience. The number of those who have at least heard of one or the other is probably on the increase, but neither term really matches the concerns or feelings of these millions. Both capitalism and socialism originated in European, and later in North American, experiences or needs. The overwhelming majority of the world's population, living in those countries commonly summarized as underdeveloped, has thus far had little use for abstract "Western" concepts.

Conversely, Western capitalism and socialism have been caught flat-footed by the emergence of the underdeveloped nations as a crucial factor in world affairs, and by the growing aspiration of these nations for a place in the sun. In the past, both capitalism and socialism had often assumed that an international division of labor would take place in the world. The expectation was that some Western nations would supply the world with textiles, machinery, and other industrial products while other countries, especially those outside Europe and North America, would produce food and raw materials for everybody.

Many countries were thus thought of as permanently earmarked for the role of a specialized supplier of such things as wheat, meat, copper, or cotton. Those countries, however, that were to undergo industrialization (a process, it is true, which in Marx' view was *ultimately* expected to affect every part of the world) were all going to follow the same general rules of economic development. There were, of course, differences in the resources and natural endowments of the various areas of the world, but none was seen in the human propensity for industrial and social progress. A population that was unfamiliar with industrial technology had to learn it, of course. But the profit motive, on one hand, and the necessity to survive by earning a wage, on the other, would take care in due course of such adjustment needs. For a more distant future, socialists anticipated the nationalization of the newly developed means of production while supporters of capitalism expected the profit system to last permanently.

The Labor and Socialist International adopted at its Milan Congress in 1951 a declaration on "Socialist Policy for the Underdeveloped Territories" which stated that, "The eradication of ex-

2

treme poverty throughout the world is as much the moral responsibility of the peoples of the more advanced countries as it is of those who live in less developed areas." The International then proposed a World Plan for Mutual Aid. On later occasions it expressed its support of a Special United Nations Fund for Economic Development (SUNFED) and discussed the burning problems of population and migration in underdeveloped areas.

But the real predicament of these areas remained alien to the traditional interests of the national parties that made up the bulk of the Socialist International. This was the chief reason, along with continuing mistrust of colonial or ex-colonial nations, why the Asian Socialist Conference constituted itself as an independent unit, though there was some overlapping.

Actually, Western socialist categories do not seem to fit the situation and needs of most underdeveloped countries any better than do Western capitalist categories. There are three basic reasons: First, what matters economically in these countries above all is the development of *new* resources, not the ownership of old ones. Underdeveloped nations are far less interested in the question of who is to own cement factories, for instance, than in the question whether or not there *is* a cement factory in the country.

Second, we know now that differences in the cultural heritage of a population may result in great variations in its economic structure and performance. A population that is imbued with the values of thrift and frugality, such as the Dutch for example, is more likely to develop capital formation and a banking system than a population which has been accustomed to immediately spend every available penny on ritual feasts or ancestral ceremonies for example. (This latter type of culture is personified by the people of Alor, Indonesia, whose ways have long intrigued anthropologists.)

Third, for related reasons some populations (the Aztecs and Balinese, for example) turned out to be more interested in basically noneconomic values such as art, religion, or war, than in the progress of industry or commerce; while other populations (the British and Americans, for example) found their greatest satisfaction in these latter pursuits. The assumption that all the people in the world desired nothing more ardently than greater riches, to be acquired by constant improvements in technology and management, turned out to be applicable in the short run, at least, only to a few cultural groups.

On the other hand, the necessary emphasis on cultural differ-

3

ences may have obscured at times certain common, or extremely widespread, needs of men: survival, reproduction, some pattern of family life, and some form of individual or group assertion and power. Allowing for cultural differences of long standing, the range of national aspirations in our period for economic and social development or a more general modernization is amazingly wide. Since the Second World War such aspirations have spread at an unprecedented pace over Asia, Africa, Latin America, and Southern Europe, although the seriousness, skill, honesty, and coordination with which they have been translated into action have differed enormously.

These aspirations differ similarly in the degree to which they rely on external aid, and in the model, if any, they propose to follow in their own economic and social development or modernization. Nearly all of these programs, however, count on much faster progress than characterized the early phases of industrialism in Great Britain, the United States, or even Japan and Russia. They usually expect to jump over the earlier steps of industrialization that were experienced by those countries. They wish to adopt immediately the most up-to-date methods of technology, management, and marketing without bothering with gradual improvements.

This is not the place to examine in detail the merits of such an approach. Certainly, however, there are decreasing indications of any desire, on the part of the modernizing countries, to simply repeat the experiences of the old industrial nations. Both capitalists and socialists in the West had assumed in the past that there would be such repetition, unless they confined themselves to the expectation of an international division of labor.

Few modernizing nations in our period count on a purely indigenous and relatively slow development along the lines of early nineteenth-century Britain. They do not rely on any spontaneous emergence of individualistic, dynamic entrepreneurs. They are in a hurry, for the indirect impact of developed economies has brought a longer life span and a growing population. At the same time, this trend is destroying the old balance (on a low level, it is true) between land resources and population. The greater the hurry, the lower the initial economic level, and the weaker the cultural tradition of individualism, the more reliance is likely to be placed by a modernizing nation on the State. The State will be expected to help create private entrepreneurs, to foster productivity in individuals or groups, perhaps with foreign aid, even to weaken the

4

retarding motivational forces that may come from an established religion or family tradition.

Modernization and -Isms

Many of the modernizing countries led by India believe rather vaguely in something they call socialism. They associate "capitalism" partly with exploitation, either colonial or native, and partly with economic chaos and inefficiency. The widespread interpretation of capitalism in contemporary America as the incorporation of individual initiative, continuous expansion of output, and ever more material comfort for the consumer, is apt to be alien to most modernizing nations. Alien also, are the underlying values of American culture such as individualism and concentration on immediate success, along with sudden shifts in intellectual interests and emotional focus. Modernizing nations often admire the dynamism and material achievement of Americans, but have little use for America itself since it is (or classifies itself as) "capitalist."

To the extent that generalizations are possible, "socialism" is interpreted in modernizing nations as three things. First, it is seen as overall government planning for the development of land resources, industries, welfare, and productivity (although the practical implementation of such plans has often been lagging behind expectations). Second, socialism involves egalitarian recognition of the "common man" as the most important object of public development policy, in contrast to the age-old deep cleavages between ruling and ruled classes and the traditional neglect of the latter by the government. Third, it means a new kind of nationalism which would bridge over regional and tribal interests and would use modernization in order to increase independence from other nations (even while there is still dire need for foreign aid). In the succinct formulation of Henry G. Aubrey, "when Indians or Burmese talk of socialism, what they mean is much closer to Western welfare capitalism than to socialism of the Communist hue."[1] To restate the point, socialism to them is not, as it is to many Western socialists, a phase of society that is to follow capitalism but an *alternative* to it in developing the economy of each country.

Labor movements in modernizing areas have been in large part a reaction to industrialization, just as they had been in Western Europe a century earlier. But, in addition, the *timing* of industrialization and the cultural background influence the kind of labor

5

organization and ideology that emerge in each country. Another influence comes from the degree and specific type of feudal traditions. Often an early, monopolistic capitalism emerges directly from feudal privileges of the few. In other cases, labor unions are faced largely with foreign capitalists or managers and react to their presence with nationalistic tendencies. These influences will be discussed in greater detail in Chapter 2.

The degree of individualism, cooperation, group coherence, and belief in explicit rules differs in the labor organizations according to the culture itself, but some generalizations concerning these organizations are possible. As a rule, they have to fight for political freedoms, just as they once had to all over Europe. This need results (in contrast to American unionism) in a generally close relationship between political and trade-unionist wings of the labor movement, and in a strong ideological commitment of both.

Their ideology usually combines some version of socialism with a quest for rapid industrialization and land reform. They need more industry in order to expand the working class and its organizations. They see little private industry that could be considered ripe for nationalization, but much need for new industrialization which they would like to see carried out by the State or, at least, coordinated in a national economic plan. They tend to assume that both industrial development and labor organization could and should be more rapid in their countries than they were in the West, and that they can leap quickly over conventional phases of development.

In their understandable impatience, many labor groups and governments in underdeveloped nations have been attracted, in varying degrees, by the example of Soviet Russia and, more recently, of Communist China. Not that they seriously mistake Soviet socialism for the kind they had in mind, nor have they, as a rule, much sympathy for totalitarian dictatorship of any kind. Occasional confusion between rapid industrial development and communist totalitarianism, it is true, has been successfully fostered by local communist parties. But what really fascinates these nations about the Russian example is, first, the speed of industrialization and the reduction of economic dependence on agriculture; and, second, the fact that these have been achieved during the last fifty years without foreign aid and, indeed, in the face of almost universal international hostility.

Many people realized that even in a country of Russia's size and background such industrial expansion could have been carried out

6

only at the price of untold suffering for many, and that this model might not be applicable or desirable elsewhere. But Russia stood as a symbol of rapid economic development on a collective basis and of hostility against Western imperialism.

With the important exception of China, no sweeping demonstration effects on newly developing countries have resulted from this initial attraction of Soviet planning (and even China is going its own way economically and otherwise). Considerable uncertainty remains in these countries concerning the extent to which the U.S.S.R. can or will actually supply large-scale aid, or the extent to which this possibility can be utilized successfully in negotiations with the West. The various purges and reforms in the communist nations since Stalin's death have also played a part in sobering the modernizing countries.

The three main features of their aspirations that were mentioned earlier (governmental development planning, prime concern with the common man, and use of modernization for greater national independence) are likely to continue for a long time, in varying forms. No matter what phraseology will be used in this process, little genuine similarity will exist between the policies of these nations and either socialism or capitalism in the Western sense. Neither capitalism nor socialism in Great Britain, Germany, or the United States had really foreseen the needs, roles, or aspirations of that great underdeveloped majority of the world's population. That is why no interpretation of today's world can be complete or realistic if the social sciences continue to use an analytic language which originated in purely Western experience.

The developed West, however, does share with its poorer brethren in Asia, Africa, Latin America, and Southern Europe a challenge which may not yet have reached its peak. It is the threat and lure of totalitarian methods that might be used in order to speed up economic development or growth. Even if the Russian and Chinese examples should not be imitated in their ideological aspects in Indonesia, Guatemala, or Egypt, they could tempt some local leaders, conceivably out of initially praiseworthy motives, to attempt fast modernization on the basis of a totalitarian regime. Such an attempt could be either of the communistic or the fascistic variety, with all the usual trimmings: elimination of political opposition and public discussion, mobilization and organization of the mob in support of official slogans and hatreds, and eventually some form of forced labor to speed up economic projects.

The entire phenomenon of totalitarianism had not been foreseen by the intellectual fathers of both capitalism and socialism in the West. In fact, not very many people in the Western countries fully understand this sad twentieth-century innovation even today, and that part of it which they usually understand least is its attraction for modernizing nations.

Cruel blows have been dealt to the old assumptions of European, and later American, supporters of either capitalism or socialism — the assumptions that the West had a natural or historical claim to world leadership, that the West could either continue to draw on the resources and labor of poorer countries or serve eventually as a model for their own development, and that rationality and democracy would prevail all over the world sooner or later. The modernizing nations today are in a great hurry, they have serious doubts about the applicability to their own situation and needs of Western experiences, and they see examples of nations which have carried out rapid industrial development with totalitarian methods.

The Lure of Totalitarianism

Among the many delusions which Western capitalism and socialism shared in the nineteenth and early twentieth centuries, the belief in the essentially rational nature and behavior of individuals, classes, and nations had perhaps the most far-reaching consequences. When communism and fascism appeared on the scene after the First World War, they met a society that was utterly unprepared for and lacking in understanding of the whole phenomenon of totalitarianism.

Historians can point out, of course, that related trends have existed in earlier phases of society. Since his beginnings, man has frequently been convinced that there is only one truth and that, consequently, everything else is untruth and should not be allowed. The existing authority has been seen as the sole administrator of that unique truth and, therefore, as the only legitimate and undisputed authority. The outstanding representative of this conviction was the mediaeval church. In a more recent period, the Bonapartism of Napoleon III in mid-nineteenth-century France demonstrated that it was possible for an autocratic regime to solicit and obtain support from the broad masses through demagogic propaganda.

Yet twentieth-century totalitarianism turned out to have some very special and unprecedented traits. To begin with, it followed a

8

period that saw itself as the heir of Enlightenment: a period that was very confident that all of mankind was on its way toward progress and freedom. Present-day totalitarianism, unlike its forerunners, cannot claim ignorance of any intellectual or social alternative. Many of the people who succumbed to it had *known* freedom to some degree, and had rejected it. Further, totalitarianism has afflicted both economically advanced and underdeveloped countries; it is in the latter that its lure appears to be greatest today for the reasons outlined earlier.

What exactly is totalitarianism? Generally speaking, a monopoly (or intended monopoly) of power over people's intellectual, emotional, economic and political resources. Totalitarianism means the exclusion of any criticism, of any questioning or scrutiny concerning the leader, regime, or social order. It means the elimination of any possible alternative, even in people's thoughts. In the face of this fundamental quality, the differences between various types of totalitarianism — the fascist, communist, or any other type — immediately recede into the background. This remains true even though these differences have time and again been stressed by each totalitarian group in its claim to be the one and only way to national and perhaps international salvation.

In order to understand the different impact of totalitarianism on economically advanced and underdeveloped nations, it is helpful to distinguish between various possible *levels* of totalitarianism which overlap but are not identical. The first such level concerns the totalitarian individual; the second refers to the totalitarian movement or group, and the third to the totalitarian regime.

The totalitarian individual may occur in any type of society, including the democratic. The totalitarian individual is emotionally incapable of tolerating any challenge to his own ideas or beliefs. He perceives such challenge as a threat to his own person. In other words, he is so profoundly insecure that he cannot stand the thought of anyone disagreeing with him. Out of uncontrollable fear, he becomes a little would-be tyrant, and he interprets this supposed threat to himself as a threat to his nation, his religion, or any other set of social values. Whoever argues with him can only be a fool or a knave, preferably the latter.

The second level of totalitarianism, the totalitarian movement or group, is reached when totalitarian individuals appear on the social scene in sufficient numbers (and with enough intensity of emotional excitement) to band together in a storm troop, political party, business association, labor union, or church. The formerly

9

scattered and isolated individuals with totalitarian traits have now found (or made up) a common cause to fight for. They must save the nation from the rascals, traitors, or exploiters who have been selling it down the river. Whoever is not with the movement is against it and therefore deserves to be cowed or destroyed by its knights. *They* hold all the answers, they are the salt of the earth; they look down, sometimes with pity but more often with contempt or hate, on those who have not yet seen the light.

The third level of totalitarianism is reached when the totalitarian movement or group has been victorious, as a rule with the help of a major social disturbance such as war, inflation, or depression. The new totalitarian regime then proceeds to establish itself in power, and to erect iron barriers against any alternative. The way of change is barred by an imposing power apparatus which includes a permanent political monopoly of the party in power by means of secret police and concentration camps, and which eliminates even the discussion of any intellectual alternative to the ruling doctrine.

The regime pictures itself as all-powerful, all-wise, all-good (except to villains), and eternal so that any attempt to uproot it would be foolish, dastardly, and hopeless. At the same time, the regime never runs out of scoundrels. The villains may be individuals or entire groups, such as classes or races, against whom the full venom of totalitarian propaganda is unloosed. If no plausible villains can be found at home, then there is always a perennial enemy abroad who conspires with other "inferior" races or classes in order to attack the "superior" one. It may sooner or later be necessary to stage a preventive attack on this enemy before he can carry out his sinister designs. Such an attack will also have the incidental effect of once more unifying a nation which may have begun to tacitly question the benefits of the totalitarian regime.

The preceding generalizations are derived from actual experiences during the last few decades in Nazi Germany, Soviet Russia, and elsewhere, but are obviously subject to variations in each concrete case. The question which poses itself in this connection is whether the dynamics of totalitarianism, as described, apply equally to its two chief brands in our period, fascism and communism; and if so whether we might not disregard, for the purpose of this discussion, any subtle differences between the two, and also the more recently emerging diversity among communist regimes.

Fascism and communism are different in their origins but similar in their results. A communist regime starts out as a proletarian

10

revolution which emphasizes mass solidarity, social equality, and internationalism. A fascist regime begins as a middle and upper class revolution, with mob support, which proclaims the superiority or supremacy of its own nation, race, or leader and, if the country concerned is of sufficient size and resources, the glory of conquest and war.

Once the two types of totalitarian regime have been installed in power, however, they soon become indistinguishable in many respects. Secret police, torture, concentration camps, forced labor, an ever-growing bureaucracy, corruption, formation of new wealth or class distinctions with the help of absolute political power, war preparations, and foreign adventures come to characterize both types. This becomes increasingly true even though their economic set-up (or, at least, phraseology) remains different — collective ownership of the means of production in one case and regimented private ownership in the other.

Actually, even this difference tends to decrease as time goes on: the communist regime may permit some peasant ownership of garden plots and livestock, for example, and may decentralize its industrial management as well, while the fascist regime may gradually step up governmental regimentation behind a façade of private ownership. During the thirties there was a story in circulation about a conversation between a Soviet Russian peasant and a Nazi German peasant, during which the Russian said, "If I had a cow the government would come and take it away," whereupon the German replied, "We are much better off indeed. If I had a cow, the government would let me keep the cow, and would let me milk it. Then it would come and take the milk away."

Old dividing lines between -isms according to the system of ownership have lost much of their significance among totalitarian regimes, no less than among democratic orders. Communism, which seemed to be a radical version of socialism and still uses this term whenever it suits its purposes, has turned out to be a world apart from the Western types of socialism. Fascism usually started out with the support of capitalist groups and pretended to protect the principle of private property from the wicked collectivists, but wound up with ruthless regimentation of private property and sometimes with its wholesale destruction in the course of a war that fascist aggressiveness had brought about.

The dividing line today must be drawn according to the freedom content of each system. Admittedly the concept of freedom is more elusive now than ever before, since all the totalitarianisms have misused it extensively. Yet it is by no means impossible to define freedom clearly. By freedom is meant here the intellectual willingness and emotional ability of an ideological movement, political group, or regime to listen to others, to weigh honestly their arguments, to take criticism from others, and to accept the possibility of temporary reverses, even prolonged exclusion from power, if the prevailing mood of the citizens and voters requires it.

Freedom thus defined constitutes a far more meaningful yardstick of social orders in our time than ownership. And according to this yardstick, the real dividing line today runs between freedom and totalitarianism — between democratic capitalism and socialism on one side of the fence, and totalitarian fascism and communism on the other. This clearly is a far cry from the frequent notion in the West that every noncommunist regime is automatically "free." The concept of the Free World has often been used semantically in a most peculiar way to include, for example, the brutal dictatorships of Francisco Franco in Spain, Rafael Trujillo in the Dominican Republic, and Syngman Rhee in Korea.

Freedom and Power

Compared with the mortal threat from fascism and communism to the fundamental freedom to think, discuss, criticize, err, and change an approach to a social task, the differences in degree, expression, or method between Western pro-capitalists and pro-socialists concerning the relationship between the government and the economy pale immediately. The ultimate similarity between communism and fascism, despite the bloodthirsty threats they keep exchanging is evidenced by the frequency with which totalitarian-minded individuals in various countries have switched their allegiance from one brand of totalitarianism to another. This has been especially true of a long array of ex-communists who overnight became right-wing extremists without at all changing their basically totalitarian frame of mind.

There is another difference, however, between freedom and totalitarianism as political principles, and it is in their relationship to power. For free ideological movements, regardless of whether they favor capitalism or socialism, the basic purpose of persuasion, propaganda, and the wooing of citizens and voters is to induce them to support the economic and social ideas of the group con-

12

cerned — so that this group can mold national policy in accordance with its program. If the majority of the people refuses to go along, the group will regretfully wait for another chance later on. If the group cannot by itself find sufficient support, it may team up, compromise, or coalesce with other groups or parties and settle for far less than it had originally hoped to achieve.

All this is an utterly impossible procedure for totalitarian groups, except as a tactical device of doubtful duration and sincerity. They want power — exclusive, unqualified, and permanent power. Everything they do or think is rooted in this one purpose. They are psychologically incapable of settling for less. If they try to, they split or perish before long, for their totalitarian-minded followers will smell treason or corruption. Totalitarian groups have to keep up their everything-or-nothing dynamism because this is the only way in which they know how to function.

It is of fundamental importance to realize the nature of the chief threat of totalitarianism in the future. The Western countries, regardless of whether they consider themselves essentially capitalistic of socialistic, offer an incomparably less fertile breeding ground for totalitarianism than do the underdeveloped areas of Asia, Africa, and Latin America. In contrast to Marx' expectation that communism — one must distinguish between the meaning of this term during his period and its meaning now — would first come to "ripe," industrialized countries, it has actually only conquered backward, essentially pre-capitalist and pre-industrial areas. The exceptions were Czechoslovakia and Eastern Germany where communism came under the pressure of Soviet armies.

Any kind of coexistence between the United States and the Soviet Union in the future will probably be of a competitive nature. And the chief theatre of operations in such a long-range competition will be the economies and governments of the modernizing nations. Such competition will far exceed a mere supply of funds. It will of necessity include technical aid for land use, transportation, communications, energy, public health, education, housing, population policy, industrialization, and trade. It may also call for substantial investment from foreign funds, either national or international. It will draw on the economic experience of more developed countries yet will require genuine sympathy, cultural understanding, and a good deal of tact, even short-run sacrifice. Whichever country comes out on top in this competition for the socio-economic guidance of newly modernizing nations may well win them over also for democracy or totalitarianism. The competition will not be confined to the United States and Soviet Russia for very long; just as Great Britain in the late nineteenth century lost its initial industrial advantage to others, both the U.S. and Soviet Russia will very soon be seriously challenged by Communist China and other industrial newcomers.

Conclusion

The totalitarian lure to modernizing nations is rooted, first of all, in the actual example of the Soviet Union which has managed to transform itself within a few decades from a backward peasant country into a leading industrial and scientific power. Second, it is based on a belief that communism helps in the fight against the upper classes of their own countries, such as the big land-owners, who have traditionally impeded any economic progress of the masses. Third, the lure appears in the anti-colonial and anti-imperialist phraseology of the Soviet Union, which is not always recognized as a mere cover-up for the new Russian imperialism and colonialism. Fourth, it is based on the impatience of poorer nations in our period to get on rapidly with modernization; to their mind, centralized planning based on a strong government promises the greatest speed.

Western-type democracy, with which most of these nations have had no practical experience, often appears to them as a cloak for an exploitative, imperialist system or, at best, as an inefficient, wasteful bickering of political power groups. Sometimes democracy is interpreted as a remote ideal toward which underdeveloped nations might strive at some future date, *after* pulling themselves out of their present economic poverty and social misery.

We mentioned earlier the rather narrow limits within which the original Marxian thinking can be of any help in understanding the present-day world. But this intellectual limitation does not alter the crucial fact that one-third of the world's population, largely in underdeveloped or newly developing areas, is ruled by people who fanatically believe in a totalitarian re-interpretation of Marxism. This very belief has become one of the most influential driving forces in contemporary history, without regard to how desperate Marx might be, were he still alive, about such unexpected social and political effects of his teachings.

It is all very well for Westerners to preach "Free Enterprise" to everybody according to their own gospel, or to say that the less

14

developed nations are wrong, or short-sighted, in being attracted by a totalitarian mirage. They certainly *are* wrong if they succumb to it. Moreover, a good many of them have thus far managed to resist the lure. But China and various smaller nations present a serious warning to the West. Entire populations of the less developed type may sooner or later succumb to the temptation of left-wing or, possibly, right-wing totalitarianism unless they find in time more promising solutions for their problems.

Some observers, it is true, believe that the threat of totalitarianism is actually greater in certain Western countries. The economic development and democratic experience of these countries have not prevented the emergence and, in some cases the rise to political power positions, of individuals and groups with definitely totalitarian traits and aspirations. Such a rise has been possible only when they were supported by a sizable number of totalitarian-minded individuals of lesser stature among the general population. Totalitarian phenomena in a Western society are more likely to be of the right-wing than of the left-wing type, and they are not rooted in economic needs of a lasting, objective nature that seem to call for strong, dictatorial measures and institutions.

In Western nations with comparative wealth and democratic background, the emergence of totalitarian individuals in substantial numbers, and their possible rise to power, is rooted in a substantial incidence of warped personalities. Such an incidence may indeed be furthered, in the last analysis, by certain psycho-economic traits of developed societies — such as new forms of uncontrollable insecurity, a phenomenon that will be discussed in later chapters. Conversely, such warped types as exist in a less developed country may find their best opportunities for rise to influence and power when a totalitarian regime is established in the early stages of modernization. Even so, it is essential to recognize the far reaching difference between rich and poor nations in regard to the roots, nature, and prospects of the totalitarian lure.

CHAPTER 2

Social Reform Movements in Modernizing Areas

How have the various social movements that exist in many modernizing areas reacted, both on the political and the emotional levels, to the challenge of modernization on the one hand, and to the authoritarian and sometimes totalitarian lure on the other? This is the subject of the present chapter.

In the terminology used here, social reform movements represent a broad concept which includes not only reform in the sense of gradual progress but also protest and revolution to the extent that they aim toward bringing about major changes in economic society. The emphasis will be on movements, not on ideologies or theories of social change. Materials from Latin America will be used chiefly, though some comparative examples from Asia and Africa will be included. The reason for the Latin American emphasis is only partly rooted in the principal sources of the author's own experience. Most Latin American nations have enjoyed political independence longer than nearly all African and many Asian nations, and some of the problems to be discussed here are in sharper focus in Latin America than anywhere else.

The first and longest part of the chapter is concerned with fundamental factors and trends, the prevailing "format," and common traits, as well as some significant differences that have influenced social reform movements in modernizing societies. The second part points out a number of alternative models of such movements and then discusses a variety of organizational forms and action methods. The third part draws some conceptual conclusions from the preceding discussion on the meaning of eco-

16

nomic systems in our period (a more elaborate analysis of this problem is presented in chapter 7).

Fundamental Factors and Common Traits

Continuing Protest against Colonialism

Typically, social reform movements, as well as many other currents of politics and thought, in modernizing areas continue to protest against colonialism long after national sovereignty has been achieved. In fact, such protest can be revived a century or more after a declaration of independence, as the example of various Latin American nations shows.

In countries where national sovereignty is of recent date, two factors are especially influential in the anti-colonialist protest: first, the fast disappearance of an illusion of national unity among revolutionists, traditionalists, and other groups from the days of common effort against a colonial oppressor; and, second, the frequent dependence on economic and administrative support by the former colonial power years after its rule has officially ended. Conspicuous examples of such a post-colonial situation are offered by most of the former French possessions in West Africa, and by Western Samoa which, since achieving political independence in early 1962, has continued to depend on New Zealand for economic aid, many top administrators, and diplomatic representation in the outside world.

This paradoxical situation tends to result in national feelings of frustration, in contrast to the exuberant expectations at the time of political liberation; and to produce, at times, severe anxieties which often find their outlet in explosive forms of social protest focused on domestic or foreign scapegoats. This trend is further accentuated by the demonstration effect of the developed countries, including the former colonial power: movies and visitors seem to emphasize to the liberated people that the well-being of the Western Europeans and North Americans has increased in this period of world-wide anti-colonialism, while their own economic headaches have frequently grown since liberation — this, of course, is not an argument against the latter. The resulting frustrations are often displaced into internal hatreds: the continued anti-colonial protest becomes a source of mutual accusations and class or race dissension at home. The potential energies of the new nation and its social reform movements are thus channeled away from funda-

17

mental changes or a genuine social revolution. As a consequence, such a revolution has been fairly ineffective in modernizing economies except for the giant nations, Russia and China.

Although the anti-colonialist protest can continue (or be revived, often aiming at a *new* target) even a century or two after political liberation, the forms of such protest in our period are likely to differ from the original. It tends to concentrate on a neocolonialism which is usually associated with economic domination by foreign interests and their domestic allies such as the big landowners. Independence thus changes its conceptual emphasis from politics to *economics*: a nation which has long had its own flag, army, constitution, and embassies can still feel (or be made to feel by an effective protest movement) that it is dominated by a concentrated economic power complex in which foreign interests are the decisive element.

A movement for social reform will then be focused on perceived economic factors that prevent the nation from building up real independence: most frequently and emphatically, on the lack of industrial development and exposure to the fluctuations of world commodity markets for primary products. Both of these impediments are typically blamed on the industrialized nations and the foreign investment capital which they provide. These nations are thought to have prevented, in their own selfish interest, the industrialization or balanced development of production, transportation network, and exports of the country, to have concentrated on the exploitation of irreplaceable resources of the soil, and to have kept down world market prices for coffee, sugar, copper, and other primary goods on which they have *made* the underdeveloped economies depend for their export earnings and import capacity.

The social protest tends to be focused on foreign interests in a two-fold way: their influence is felt to impede the development of a more stable and prosperous economy precisely at a time when the example of rising living standards in the wealthier countries is raising the level of aspirations in the modernizing nations. The protest movements in the latter, therefore, tend to be characterized by a voluntarist spirit of impatience. They are unwilling to rely either on a market automatism with anticipated *long-range* effects of an international division of labor, or on a static interpretation of the world economy assigning to the less developed nations a permanent role as exporters of primary products. Reliance on inexorable laws of historical change does not appeal to them even when their phraseology is colored by liberalism or Marxism.

A different but somewhat related variety of movements for "real" independence is focused on education, rather than economic development, although the latter is often understood to be largely dependent upon the former. Without widespread popular education, political independence is seen as a mere façade for actual domination by foreign interests allied with a small domestic oligarchy.

Finally, discontent with the existing forms of independence may be focused on the social disorganization that usually accompanies incipient changes in economic structure. In this case the drive for modernization, with the resulting differentiation, has begun but has not brought economic independence and new social integration as promptly or fully as the social reform groups had anticipated. The protest centers mainly on the unevenness of socio-economic change in this phase of modernization. This stage includes developmental discontinuities, leading to such phenomena as the destruction of indigenous communities before a new pattern of social organization can be offered and the rapid growth of shantytowns on the fringe of large cities, populated by peasants of yesterday who are helplessly trapped between two almost unrelated phases of society and development.

Anti-Imperialism as Unifier

The anti-colonial and economic elements of the drive for "real" independence frequently merge into an anti-imperialist emphasis of social reform movements in newly developing economies. This orientation is in some cases influenced by a modified version or combination of the theories of Hobson, Lenin, and Luxemburg; imperialism is seen as a drive for *economic* domination of other nations with the use of political and military, as well as economic, methods to achieve this goal.

The historical verification of such theories or ideologies is less easy in some cases than in others, but regardless of their factual merits, they typically serve as a unifying influence within a social reform movement, and between the latter and the rest of the nation. Nothing unifies as effectively as a villain held in common (a practice which does not necessarily prove that real villains do not exist at times).

The anti-imperialist protest in our period is more often than not focused on foreign investment in the country concerned, which is seen as an exploitative and corrupting force. Commodity price fluctuations on the world market for the chief products of the

19

country, especially adverse terms of trade, are interpreted as the effect of evil intention or harmful automatism. Foreign aid to one's country also, is often viewed as part of the imperialist quest for its domination, most of all when strings are attached to the aid, or when it serves to maintain an unpopular government.

Nationalization then assumes a strong emotional, not merely an economic, significance. The concept of nationalization, which in Europe ordinarily refers to the taking over by the state of some or all the means of production from private owners in the same country, comes to mean in a modernizing economy the taking over of foreign-owned factories, lands, or mines by national interests. These interests are expected to be represented by the state; but what matters to social reform movements in these areas more than public ownership or equal distribution is the fact that these means of production (including those which did not exist in usable form before being developed by foreign groups) no longer belong to imperialists.[1]

Paradoxically, these attitudes are quite often accompanied by tolerance, if not active support, of quasi-imperialist policies of the modernizing nations themselves; at first less for economic motives (though they are not entirely absent) than for motives of territorial aggrandizement. "Anti-imperialist" Egypt occupied Yemen, Indonesia for years concentrated much of its national effort on the acquisition of West Irian, Guatemala has designs on Belice, and Venezuela on parts of Guyana — even though each of these countries has, or should have, its hands full with domestic development. This also applies to some aspects of the Kashmir dispute between India and Pakistan. Even more paradoxically, many of these nations and, most emphatically, their social reform movements, have managed to combine their anti-imperialism toward the West and their own quasi-imperialism with a neutralist position toward the major world powers. The explanation, if not justification, of such paradoxes lies in the specific patterns and emotional aspects of nationalism in the social reform movements of modernizing societies.

Variations of Meanings of Nationalism in Social Reform Movements

The most common characteristic of the nationalist element in social reform movements of the modernizing societies is a frantic search for national identity. Even the originally internationalist Marxism is often interpreted in a nationalist way, as will be shown

20

later. The reasons for this typical uncertainty about the essence and goals of national existence are threefold. First, some of the new nations (such as Congo, Indonesia, and Pakistan) had never existed as a national unit before the colonial regime and had in most cases been shaped as an administrative unit only by the foreign dominating power. Second, regional, ethnic, or religious differences, conflicts and groupings within some of these nations have a far longer and stronger tradition than national unity. Third, some of the older nations have not managed thus far to overcome the socio-cultural and economic dualism which has excluded the majority of the nation from national markets and decision-making processes (Guatemala and Equador, for example).

In addition to this universal search for national identity, the strong nationalist ingredient in social reform movements assumes a variety of characteristics in specific movements and areas.[2] These orientations range from nationalistic socialism à la Nasser, which tries to combine authoritarian planning at home with Arab nationalism toward the other Arab countries; to populist-type groups, often with redistributive, rather than productive, emphasis in their economic beliefs; to the cultural revivalism of certain movements in Latin America, with an *indigenista* orientation;[3] to democratic nationalism, exemplified by Eduardo Frei's supporters in Chile.

Nationalism in modernizing societies has many meanings. This is one reason why the uneasy and fragile "International of the Nationalists" has thus far been of interest more in terms of mentality than in terms of effectiveness. The cooperation of all the underprivileged nations, of Bandung Conference days, has been pronounced as a goal in many social reform movements but has not been implemented. Even more important, there has been an almost complete absence of *internationalist* movements among the social reform groups in newly developing economies. This has been true despite the rather far-reaching, if contradictory, impact of Marxism on these groups.

The Impact of Marxism

The question why Marxism, against the expectations of its founders, has been far more effective in pre-industrial than in highly industrialized areas, or more effective in the early phases of industrialization than later, has been discussed many times, but has never been completely resolved. The fact remains that some form — or a more or less devious interpretation — of Marxism has been influential in most social reform movements in modernizing societies, even in those which do not profess officially or systematically an adherence to the Marxist system of thought and action.

Undoubtedly, features of British capitalism in the early decades of the nineteenth century, on which Marx and Engels based a large part of their teachings, are paralleled to *some* degree in the modernizing economies of our period. There are the social rigidities and polarity of classes as the immediate aftermath of feudalism and the crudely exploitative practices of employers. But this is not the whole story of Marxist impact. In order to understand it more fully, we have to add the unity of all the social concepts which Marxism offers to a disjointed new nation and to disoriented social movements, the explanation of all social evils from a single source.

In addition, on the practical-political level, there is usually superior and persistent organizational preparation, leading to an important role of communist parties in modernizing areas, especially where an authoritarian regime confines all the non-official or opposing groups to an underground existence. Even more important, however, are the developmental examples of Russia, China and, to a far smaller degree, Cuba. Russia and China have demonstrated that industrialization and economic independence from the Western world are *possible* and that they can be achieved within a few decades if one is willing to pay the price; and they have done so on the basis of a Marxist ideology of sorts, even though they quarrel over who represents the authentic brand. In the case of Cuba, an incomparably smaller and more vulnerable country, the industrialization drive has not succeeded thus far, but social revolution, economic independence from the former dominant power and, in a limited way, modernization do offer an example expressed in a peculiar Marxist-Leninist phraseology.[4]

On the other hand, the impact of Marxism on social reform movements is limited by a realization of the tremendous difference in size and resources between Russia and China on one hand, and all other countries, with the possible exceptions of India and Brazil, on the other; by misgivings about the nature of totalitarian regimes and their failures in agrarian policy; by the conflict between Soviet communism and Chinese communism; by some continued hopes for development aid from the West; and by reluctance to accept any kind of economic determinism in the search for national identity and self-assertion. Moreover, Marxism in its traditional forms makes no real allowance for national or cultural variations within the rise of an industrial society.

The combination of nationalism and Marxism in most social reform movements in the modernizing areas represents an uneasy and unstable arrangement. Aside from the fact that this form represents a paradoxical deviation from the original, proletarian-oriented Marxism, the latter-day variety of communist tactics which relies on peasant guerilla fighters in the mountains — such as the late Ché Guevara and Camilo Torres tried to apply to the Western hemisphere — is not likely to have much impact on those social reform movements which are rooted in middle class, intellectual, or workers' groups. The basic problem of the movements under discussion is that there has been little original thinking within them, along with very little useful guidance from social movements in the developed economies.

Comparative Aspects of Social Reform Movements in the West

There are manifold reasons why Western social reform movements either through their historical experiences or in their contemporary forms, seldom provide a useful example for today's modernizing societies, even though the former may try to give financial or moral aid to the latter.

First, early social movements in England, France, Holland, Sweden, and various other countries were not up against the lack of established national identity that characterizes many of the modernizing nations today (though Germany and Italy retained some of this problem until their late political unification in the 1870s and, to some extent, even later). Likewise, the presence of an established institutional framework and of explicit cultural restraints upon the forms of group action, distinguished the Western societies and their social reform movements even during the early industrial phase from those in many of the modernizing nations today.

Second, the dynamism of the latter produces the different and more ruthless methods of a struggle for personal power *within* the new social reform movements or political parties, as well as within each modernizing nation as a whole; a struggle in which the stakes are extremely high — not only livelihood and prestige, but quite often life and family existence. The widespread shortcomings of education serve to accentuate such forms of power struggle. Little from earlier experience, and hardly anything from the more recent period of social reform movements in Western Europe and North America is thus felt to provide a usable example in this respect for the less developed areas.

Third, there is now the demonstration effect of the high standard of living that is possible in industrialized economies and of the success of Western social reform movements in making a high standard accessible to workers and farmers. In some, though not many, modernizing areas the influence of immigrants from Europe has been substantial on both counts: the Spaniards, Italians, and Germans in Chile, Uruguay, and other countries brought with them their aspirations for a better standard of living as well as the experience of Socialist or Christian reform movements in Europe.

Fourth, in their mentality and methods, the social reform movements in modernizing areas are often characterized by an impatience, violence, and volatility, which find more precedents in the early industrial, crudely exploitative phase of Western European capitalism, than in the Western development experience of recent decades. Moreover, social movements in modernizing areas today show greater consciousness of and focus on planned economic and social development, especially industrialization and land reform, than did European movements during their early phases. Last but not least, fundamental changes have occurred in the nature and meaning of both capitalism and socialism during the intervening period between the rise of Western movements for social reform and the emergence of today's movements in modernizing areas.

The Meaning of Capitalism and Socialism in Modernizing Areas

Both concepts underwent far-reaching changes in the industrially developed economies long before the quest for modernization became widespread in the rest of the world. All over Western Europe and North America the social impact of economic fluctuations — especially mass unemployment, the concentration of economic power, the social cost of slums and poor education, and the economic impact of a large-scale defense establishment — had led to far-reaching government intervention even where the phraseology of free enterprise was maintained as a kind of self-deceptive smokescreen, especially in the official business creed. At the same time, Western socialism had been profoundly affected by its own successes in achieving higher living standards for workers and, in quite a different way, by the economic and political effects of Soviet communism, which had appropriated the term socialism in an internationally confusing manner. Both capitalism and socialism had thus changed their connotations in the West almost beyond recognition before the Second World War, and even more so after it.

24

But both capitalism and socialism in the West had been caught flatfooted by the great upsurge of development aspirations in the poorer nations after the Second World War, and had little to offer them insofar as intellectual stimulation or guidance was concerned. At the same time, neither capitalism nor socialism in the Western sense were meaningful concepts to the great majority of people in less developed areas in relation to their own daily life experience as isolated, mostly illiterate peasants or laborers whose energies and interests were absorbed by the necessity to supply food for the family from day to day.

Likewise, for the small educated groups, these Western concepts (though for different reasons) have little real meaning even when such groups emulate Western phraseology. The prime problem and task in the modernizing economies is not to decide the pattern of ownership, either private or public, for the existing means of production and developed resources, but to effectively achieve development of *new* (or unutilized) resources. Moreover, development is no longer seen as the mere achievement of the living standards of North America and Western Europe, but as the overall transformation of the socio-economic, educational and, to some degree, cultural patterns from the past, as will be shown in later chapters.

The concept of socialism has thus assumed, among the more educated groups in the modernizing areas, the meaning of a more effective and less exploitative method of *development* than capitalism. Their perception of the latter is somewhat related to the exploitative and socially chaotic features of early capitalism in Western Europe, as well as to the typically monopolistic traits of many business concerns in newly developing areas. The basic difference between capitalism and socialism is not seen in absolute principles of ownership but in the method and spirit of modernization. This can be traced in Senghor's concept of African socialism and in comparable statements by Haya de la Torre and others.[5]

The decisive criterion of socialism, thus, is not seen there in the public ownership of the means of production, or in class struggle, any more than it is in Western countries today. Actually, the role of government and public administration is interpreted in a far more complex way. On the one hand, socialist protest and various other reform movements are directed in large part against chaotic and corrupt administration practices and the red tape and nepotism that characterize most of the less developed nations. On the other hand, socialist (and many nonsocialist) reform groups expect from the government the provision of an extensive infrastructure for private as well as public development, some degree of state enterprise in fields unsuitable for private ownership, credit and investment aid to business, and planning. The planning concept here is not that of a centralized, publicly owned economy, but the government supplying the overall framework, coordination, supervision, and guidance for the integrated development of agriculture, industry, regional and educational improvements, and other socio-economic activities.

All this, of course, has resulted in far-reaching ambiguity in regard to the concepts of socialism and capitalism in most of the modernizing areas and, especially, within their social reform movements. There is a widespread attitude of "we are all socialists now," in the sense of a kind of declaration of intention to encourage social justice and coordinated modernization. Such socialism is usually seen as quite compatible with a substantial, even prevailing and increasing, role for private enterprise. In the traditional, if outmoded, terminology of Western capitalism and socialism, capitalism and socialism are considered in the modernizing economies as compatible to a large degree, and such (often ill-defined) interpretations apply to the programs of many of their social reform movements.

Agrarian Reform Movements

Socialism cuts across those reform movements in modernizing areas that are focused on basic changes in agrarian conditions. Part of the difference in ideological emphasis can be explained by the great variety of agrarian forms and institutions, which range from subsistence farming and *minifundia* to semi-feudal big landownership and large-scale commercial farming (sometimes within the same country). Consequently, the rural population, whose condition a reform movement wants to improve, can consist of subsistence peasants, hired laborers, *peones* or *inquilinos*, or other rural groups; and the focus of an agrarian reform movement may be anti-feudal, anti-capitalist, cooperative, or other. The initial aims of peasant movements often simply stress the right to organize. In addition, the usual emphasis on land reform can mean primarily the expropriation and redistribution of land, the encouragement of *ejidos* or cooperatives, or rural credit, education, technical assistance, and other forms of public aid to the peasant, especially the new settler.

Any or all of these aims overlap in some countries with the

basic endeavor to incorporate into the economic, political, and cultural life of the nation certain rural groups — sometimes the majority of the population — that have traditionally been excluded from it. In Latin America, this has applied especially to the Indians of Peru, Equador, Guatemala, and Bolivia. In Bolivia and Peru some modest steps toward such incorporation have actually been made in recent years. The focus of agrarian reform movements in these cases is on the transformation of "dualistic" societies in which a large part of the rural population has traditionally been excluded from active participation in national life.

To this has been added in recent decades the problem of the new urban slum-dweller who comes from a rural background and has maintained some, slowly weakening, agricultural links. The *cholo* in the shantytowns of Lima, for instance, who is not quite an Indian any more but has not become a real Peruvian is at this point the forgotten man, who is not really represented by any social reform movement except by occasional, more or less explosive, outbursts.

Since the advent of *fidelismo* in Cuba, frequent fears have been expressed in the United States that under its influence (perhaps combined with that of Chinese communism) peasant movements, supplemented by guerilla organizations, might become the mainstay of communism in Latin America and possibly in other parts of the world. At one time, the New York Times ran a front-page story about Francisco Julião and his Peasant Leagues in the poverty-stricken Northeast of Brazil, as the supposed spearhead of Fidel Castro in South America. Other North American newspapers and reviews, including at least one of a socialist nature, followed suit, and the resulting brainwashing of the reading public aroused grim amusement in Northeast Brazil where Julião had been better known as a lawyer, large landowner, and publicity-seeking politician.[6]

Genuine agrarian reform movements in modernizing areas have thus far been rare and their effectiveness has been limited. The peasant element can however, become of substantial importance when it is incorporated into or allied with a broader movement for social reform, especially one rooted in the labor and intellectual groups of the areas concerned.

Labor Movements

The nature of labor organizations in modernizing areas is largely determined by the fact that nonfarm workers represent a mere minority in a mainly rural society, that most of them are unskilled and not fully committed to their jobs and occupations and that employment tends to fluctuate heavily. However, industrial and commercial workers, despite their poverty in absolute terms, tend to be incomparably better off, even in urban slum areas, than the rural majority of the population in villages. At the same time, industry in most of these countries has spread sluggishly and unevenly, and usually is confined to some islands in the midst or on the fringe of a vast rural majority;[7] but the industrial workers' level of aspirations often rises far more rapidly than that of the rural groups from which they usually came.

The workers' social protest is mainly centered on the early effects of industrialism and modern technology, including slum conditions and other forms of social disorganization, unsafe practices in the plant, lack of effective social legislation, inflationary disruption of real wages, and perhaps most of all, the chronic unemployment that affects a large part of the labor force either as a prevailing condition or as a constant threat. Behind these conditions is the nature of management in modernizing economies: its domination by family status needs in combination with political pull, its initial lack of expert training, its short-range view, and its casual work habits.[8] The paternalist mentality, at first welcomed by the early groups of industrial or commercial workers, becomes outmoded and arouses resistance in a somewhat later phase of modernization. Productivity attitudes, at first, are lacking in understanding from the side of manegement no less than from the workers, and the latter tend to interpret those productivity measures that are attempted as more refined methods of exploitation. Financial stabilization policies likewise tend to arouse the workers' protest.

Under these conditions, industrial relations, ideology, and politics are as a rule inextricably interwoven. The kind of labor movement that is confined to strictly economic goals is almost nonexistent in modernizing areas. Labor unions typically are dominated by a specific ideology with radical, nationalist, or religious emphasis, and are deeply involved in political action either directly or through an affiliated political party. In fact a distinction between political and more definitely economic action is often difficult to make. Strikes are as likely to be of a noneconomic as an economic nature, and very often have both aspects in some ill-defined combination. Anarchosyndicalist vestiges from Spanish or Italian sources are not infrequent in Latin America, most of all in union protest against an authoritarian political regime. In fact, labor has provided almost the only organized challenge to the political leadership of the military in various countries, although there are also a few recent examples in Latin America of a coalition between the two forces.[9] In Africa, a wide range of labor groups from company unions to semi-governmental manipulation of industrial relations can be found, but spontaneous organization of nationwide scope remains almost unknown. In many modernizing areas the protest against foreign employers, or more general anti-imperialist action, absorbs more of the unions' energies than does the quest for economic advancement of the workers.

In economic and noneconomic pursuits alike, action methods are usually characterized by a wishful thinking and voluntarism which do not perceive the existence of or necessity for restraints or conditioning limitations, either in the organization involved or in public policy. Impatient violence is extremely frequent as the best or only perceived way to get results. Similarly, impulsive and erratic procedures in the administration and financing of a labor union are very frequent, and the typical weakness of central union leadership encourages improvisation on the local or company level, to which most of the union groups are confined. Employers sometimes actually prefer to deal with strong unions that can be counted on to deliver the goods, rather than with more docile but less effective groups with a fluctuating membership. There is a dearth on all levels of labor leaders with extensive education and real vision. Those few who exist are usually far better equipped than the average worker; they often graduate into national leadership, especially in Africa, and tend to use the labor unions merely as instruments of national politics.

Perhaps it should be emphasized that there are numerous exceptions to any such generalizations and special cases which do not fit into any general pattern. The most conspicuous of these is *peronismo*, which is not exactly a labor movement in itself but has retained the allegiance of some two-thirds of the Argentine labor unions and possibly an even higher proportion of the rank-and-file workers during the decades after the downfall and exile of Perón himself. The reason for this support of course, has been the phenomenon of his being associated by organized labor with the encouragement of unionism, rising wage levels, and social legislation, as opposed to the traditional economic and political rule of the big landowners and businessmen. We need not discuss here the question whether this attitude of a large part of Argentine labor has been realistic. In any case, the specific situation which it has represented and the degree of industrial development under which it has occurred are not typical of the conditions and forms of labor movements in modernizing areas.

To what extent can labor organizations be expected to *lead* movements for social reform in modernizing areas? In none of these areas does the experience of organized labor provide a conclusive answer.[10] Above all, any spontaneous rise of genuine leaders from the ranks of labor has thus far been very limited, and quite understandably so in view of the handicaps involved. In fact, almost the only effective leadership of such movements (as earlier in some parts of Europe) has come from some type of intellectual elite.

Intellectual Elites and Social Reform Movements

The middle class or intellectual elite which assumes the role of a spokesman for voiceless downtrodden groups is not in itself a new phenomenon. What is relatively new is the composition of the intellectual groups that typically assume this role in the social reform movements of modernizing nations, and their attitude toward the outside world.

As in the past, the intelligentsia in these countries is often Western-educated; but there is now a more recent element composed of those trained technically and ideologically in Soviet Russia and, less frequently thus far, in Communist China. There is also a growing group of those who were educated in a somewhat more advanced country of the same area, for example, Iraquis in Egypt or Peruvians in Chile. The Western-educated group, which remains the largest by far, is split into two segments: those who are greatly impressed by what they saw and learned in the West and sometimes become rigid protagonists of conventional wisdom acquired abroad, and those who only found their anti-imperialist preconceptions confirmed. In any case, the traditional prevalence of *abogados* or people with a humanistic background among the educated has slowly been giving way to the growing significance of those with technical or specialized training, who see their country and its reform needs in terms quite different from those of the older group.

Among the intellectual groups, the university students no longer only come from the upper classes, and they have assumed an ever more active role in political and social confrontations. This, it is true, only applies to a small militant minority. The majority find the acquisition of technical knowledge according to either the Western or the Soviet example (often combined with making a living), too absorbing to allow them to take a leading part in social protest or political events, but they rarely oppose the others actively. This leading role of the students in public affairs, which in some places has come to include high school students, appears primarily in Latin America but includes some of the Arab countries and parts of Asia and Africa. Its forms have ranged from demonstrations and strikes to armed revolt and guerilla warfare.

Some of the student participation and leadership in social reform movements are reminiscent of the *Narodniki* in Russia during the latter part of the nineteenth century and of some populist currents in the Western world. But there is an important qualification: the influence of the students in the modernizing areas today is based in large part on local interpretations of university autonomy, which not merely serve the cause of academic freedom but in some countries permit student groups to seize complete control of the universities, including faculty and staff appointments, and the use of university premises as bulwarks of political movements. It remains to be seen whether future university reforms in these countries will be confined to changes in curriculum and education methods, or whether they will include a revised interpretation of the students' general role in the university and the nation.

Aside from university students, various layers of urban, rural, and semi-educated (sometimes intellectually rootless) middle class groups have in various ways provided leadership or, at least, a voice for agrarian and labor movements. A special case of elite leadership in social reform is presented by recent Church-led currents in Latin America favoring social change, and the incipient and still quite spotty transformation of the clergy from a traditional factor of reaction into a reform influence. More generally, there are also some uncertain indications that the pattern of social leadership by the various groups which enjoy better education than the great majority will be re-interpreted in the future in terms of greater emphasis on more and better education in the nation at large.

The Authoritarian Reformer

It is the educated or semi-educated groups that frequently produce that peculiar phenomenon in modernizing areas, the authoritarian reformer who attempts to combine mass support for major changes with a charismatic one-man rule, and regards his rule as socialism. In this last respect one might cite Hitler's National Socialism as a precedent but the comparison fails in more than one respect. It really only applies to the desperate need for unity and a symbol of national identity: in Germany because of the long delay in its unification during the nineteenth century, and in the modernizing countries of our period because of the illusion of unity from the days of a common fight for political liberation which tends to disappear soon after independence has been achieved.

The authoritarian leader is not necessarily identified with spearheading the past fight for independence, although he may emerge from its militant group. The qualities required during this fight are in large part destructive; the external enemy must be hit as hard as possible. Sustained modernization after the achievement of independence, and the mobilization of mass energies in its support, require constructive qualities. The guerilla leader of yesterday rarely possesses the economic understanding and broad organizational gifts that are required for industrialization, although he may be quite unwilling to admit such limitations or may feel that what industrialization needs most is strong national leadership with or without economic and managerial knowledge.

The authoritarian leader invariably organizes a reform movement in his support, most often in the form of a political mass party which assumes monopolistic privileges. Without holding a brief for any one-party system, we need to understand its positive function in modernizing areas and the reasons for its frequency. The amorphous characteristics of a nation aspiring to develop quickly yet lacking in coherence and organization — the same traits that lead to the rise of an authoritarian leader — result in a widely felt need for some organization of the social process, especially in a new nation. The single party then is interpreted as the best, perhaps the only possible way to do so. Initially, the single party is not necessarily the mere tool of an authoritarian leader, though it frequently becomes one in practice. The single party may admit ideological or socio-economic groupings *within* its ranks, sometimes functional groupings of workers or students, for example, but it will not tolerate competition from other parties in organizing the nation or from a specific movement for social change.

The relations between party hegemony and the degree of political and organizational freedom are not always well-defined. In the

32

cases of PRI (Partido Revolucionario Institucional) in Mexico, the PPD (Partido Popular Democrático) in Puerto Rico, and the Congress Party in India, the leading party has not been based on an authoritarian one-man rule or an institutionalized monopoly; but the intended unifying functions of the party in question, especially in mobilizing and organizing mass energies in the process of modernization, have been unmistakable. In the case of Mexico, at least, the self-perpetuating traits of the government party are obvious even though its authoritarian or personalist features are weaker.

Opposition movements have a much harder time, and are interpreted quite differently, in modernizing areas than in countries with more sophisticated economic and political institutions. Opposition, at least outside the institutional framework of the ruling party, is thought of as a national, not an individual, concept. It is clear that whatever may be the historical explanation of such interpretations, they lend themselves only too easily to brutal, self-perpetuating misuse by an authoritarian dictator.

In extreme cases, to mention only Nkrumah in Ghana and Duvalier in Haiti, such authoritarian rule has assumed a totalitarian character. In modernizing nations, its features are likely to differ from those of European fascism and communism but it may take over from them some techniques of oppression. A mass movement in support of the totalitarian ruler and, especially, his development program for the nation, may be organized from above, although Duvalier never bothered to do that and just let the economy stagnate. The totalitarian social-reform movement focussed on modernization goals and fostered from the top characterizes this variety of the groupings that are discussed here.

The Military and Social Reform Needs

The authoritarian dictator in a modernizing country may or may not be rooted in the military hierarchy. At any rate, the two things should not be confused, and an active role by the military in politics, reform, or development planning does not necessarily mean authoritarianism. There is a long way, with many relapses, from the old fashioned *caudillo* to the revolutionary or developmental reformer in uniform. Moreover, the broader social basis and partial professionalization of the military hierarchy in *some* modernizing areas, partly under the influence of foreign military aid, has had certain moderating effects on the socio-economic, poli-

33

tical, and developmental role of the military without, indeed, eliminating all the dangers.

When the military takes the reigns of a nation into its hands, such rule is seen by many people and reform groups as autocratic but unifying; the military is perceived (or perceives itself) as the only available force of coherence in a nation with weak civilian institutions, and thus is seen as the representative of nationalism in the sense of symbolizing national identity. Especially is this true of dualistic societies; the military in Peru, for instance, boasts that it had taught Indian boys Spanish, reading and writing and various crafts long before anyone else seriously attempted to do so.

More than that, the military often sees itself, and is seen by others, as the real guiding force, referee, or caretaker among conflicting civilian groups and among movements for social reform.[11] In fact, the military today tends to interpret itself as the natural (or only possible) spearhead of modernization, if not revolution. The regime of Marshal Castelo Branco in Brazil, for example, constantly referred to itself as revolutionary. The stated purpose of such military regimes is to carry through necessary public works and industrialization, to stop inflation, to modernize the economy, and to encourage popular education, all with the expected support of a popular movement designed to back up the military regime. The old adage that "one cannot sit on bayonets" is far more on the minds of military rulers in our period than it was on the minds of their *caudillo* predecessors, although some of the latter still remain.

Another pattern of the military stepping in to resolve an acute crisis and then to groom civilian groups who can take over after a while — and it remains to be seen whether this historical pattern is still in effect — can be seen in the examples of Egypt, Indonesia, Congo, Peru, and Bolivia. In these countries the military has attempted in one way or other to establish a national coherence, to chase out earlier autocratic or corrupt leaders and parties, and to get the nation on its way to modernization. In each case, the military regime has tried to build up a mass movement in its support, and to preserve a way back to civilian rule for some ill-defined future. Actually, the danger of a self-perpetuating military rule with either spontaneous or artificially built up backing by a mass movement is considerable. There are various other drawbacks to this contemporary phenomenon: the almost inevitable restrictions of civil liberties and political freedom, the internal factionalism among the military, which may sooner or later destroy the appearance of unity that gave the regime its original *raison d'être*, and even the emergence of an authoritarian dictator who transforms himself from a civilian or a subaltern officer into a generalissimo (as Batista once did in Cuba and Mobutu did in the Congo more recently). Moreover, the social reform goals and the spontaneous or artificial mass movement in their support are easily eroded in the course of a military regime, and what is left is autocracy, if not totalitarianism, usually with some fascist traits.

It is true that full-fledged fascist movements and trends in Europe and North America have been rooted in certain socio-economic and psychological characteristics of *industrialized* societies. These include widespread insecurity feelings in the upper and middle classes; fear of radical or labor movements; economic disruption caused by business fluctuations, especially by inflation, mass unemployment, or a sequence of both; aftereffects of a major war or perceived national humiliation; or other disturbing factors in a society which *has* known wealth, power, and freedom but has suffered a setback of some kind. Moreover, very few of the successful fascist movements were led by a military figure. In various respects, the military regimes of modernizing areas do not particularly fit the pattern of Western fascism, and in fact both military and civilian autocracies in these areas and their supporting mass movements now like to use a socialist, even Marxist, phraseology.

Some fascist elements, however, can be found in these autocracies and movements, as represented at various times by the *Integralistas* in Brazil, the *Sinarquistas* in Mexico, and the *Falange* in Bolivia, while Peronism in Argentina, despite its aggressive nationalism and the military background of the dictator, is closer to the Bonapartist than to the fascist pattern, insofar as we wish to use any European comparisons. In short, despite the presence of *some* fascistic elements in certain protest or reform movements in modernizing areas, such as extreme nationalism, the emergence of would-be Führers, and mass or mob support for them, the concept of fascism does not fit these movements particularly well, nor should military rule as such be confused with fascism or autocracy.

Foreign Aid and Social Reform Movements

Finally, what has been the mutual impact of foreign aid, either developmental or other, and social reform movements in modernizing areas? In both directions, there has been a peculiar mixture

35

of endorsement and mistrust. To most social reform movements in these areas, foreign aid, especially from the United States, is suspect out of the anti-colonialist, anti-imperialist, and nationalist mentality that was discussed earlier. Foreign aid is often thought of as being essentially in the economic or moral interest of the nation that grants it, or at best of the uppermost layers of the receiving nation; and as being a tool of subjugation of the latter to the investment and foreign policy interests of wealthier countries. But at the same time, the protest and reform groups, often complain about the inadequacy of aid programs, and demand *more* support from the wealthy nations, especially for development purposes.

The same ambivalence has characterized congressional and administrative attitudes in the United States toward social reform movements in modernizing areas. On the one hand, land reform, tax reform, and development planning are considered a requirement in order to make aid effective, especially under the Alliance for Progress; on the other hand, social reform movements with very similar aims, especially land reform or any degree of public or cooperative ownership of enterprises, are suspected of being communist-inspired. Such suspicions, of course, often play into the hands of the real Communists.

The latter, it is true, have rarely been able to benefit politically from Soviet aid to their countries, such as has been granted to Egypt and India. The days are gone when Soviet policy was either clumsy enough to use such methods for *direct* political penetration in the party sense or inept enough to give this impression. The Soviet technicians who are sent to these countries now belong to a different intellectual generation, and the receiving governments draw a careful line between the two kinds of Communists. Moreover, the split between Russian and Chinese communism has made the direct use of communist parties in these countries for the purposes of Soviet foreign policy substantially more difficult. The chief expectation is that the industrial and technological example of the Soviet Union's achievements and the aid it is now capable of offering will influence social movements in the receiving countries indirectly in the way desired by the Soviets.

Regardless of the source of foreign aid, there is bound to be a clash sooner or later with the quest for nationalist self-assertion, which characterizes practically all the social reform movements in modernizing societies. From the viewpoint of the aid-granting nations, therefore, they are likely to find less and less readiness to receive foreign aid unless it is supplied through international channels such as United Nations agencies, and perhaps even this method will eventually lose its viability. This problem will be further discussed in Chapter 8.

Alternative Models and Action Methods

Orientations of Models

The preceding discussion can be summarized in a number of alternative models of social reform movements in modernizing areas. Perhaps it should be emphasized that in historical reality such movements invariably represent a *combination* of two or more elements from the list that follows. The actual differences, therefore, are not of an absolute character but represent variations in the respective emphasis of each type of movement.

Labor

The movement concerned is rooted in labor unions whose membership is largely unskilled and fluctuating The starting point of activities is the improvement of working conditions and mitigation of the effects of a new industrial technology, but this is combined with political and ideological aims of a voluntarist and violent disposition.

Marxism

The lodestar of this kind of movement is the interpretation of the world in terms of class struggle and of an inevitable showdown between a decaying imperialist world and rising revolutionary forces which represent the only hope for a desirable type of modernization. Nationalism and Marxism are considered natural allies in the fight for revolutionary goals, although party communism is not necessarily seen as the best way of implementing such goals.

Peasants

Since all the underdeveloped economies are basically agrarian, this type of movement considers the peasants and rural laborers the natural mainstay of any effective movement for social reform. Moreover, only a basically rural movement is seen as offering hope for the incorporation of the culturally and economically isolated peasant population into the national economy and society.

Students

In this case university students see themselves as the kind of intellectual elite that can best lead a revolutionary movement. For a mass base in the labor or peasant classes, the students feel they should be the articulate spokesmen. University autonomy is interpreted and used as an instrument of such revolutionary leadership.

Nationalism

The emphasis is on unifying factors in the search for national identity, and on real independence achieved through basic socio-economic changes, especially industrialization. This includes elements of cultural revivalism and populism, along with desire for some cooperation among the nationalist movements in the various modernizing areas.

Charisma

A strong leader who serves as the symbol or incorporation of national identity and as organizer of a single party designed to represent the whole nation, is the focus of this orientation. A single political organization, with possible leeway for discussion *within* this organization, gives the strong leader his forum and instrument, and opposition to leader and party is construed as an anti-national attitude.

Totalitarianism

In its extreme form, a charismatic orientation can lead to totalitarianism, usually with some fascist elements even when the phraseology used is partly socialist. Such totalitarianism is interpreted as the only effective method leading toward modernization under the conditions of a society stricken by poverty and foreign exploitation.

Church

This type of social refoi . movement is mainly confined to Latin America and is a fairly new occurrence in comparison to the traditional anti-reform attitude of the Catholic Church. The new emphasis is on the interpretation of Christian values in terms of basic social changes and on a new approach to socio-economic needs on the part of the major groups in society, including the upper classes.

Development

This orientation represents a considerable variety of foci ranging from the Christian Democrats in South America to *Mapai* in Israel, and it overlaps with some of the approaches mentioned before. In each case, the emphasis in the social reform movement concerned is not on negative but on positive goals, more specifically on the socio-economic development of the nation as the only real answer to its traditional problems and limitations.

Organizational Forms and Action Methods

The organizational forms and action methods of social reform movements in modernizing countries cut across all the models just listed, and the mix of forms and methods in each is subject to great variations. Moreover, the frequent similarity of certain outward forms of behavior should not be allowed to obscure fundamental differences among them in regard to the content of their aims and their underlying mentality.

Actually, the types of social reform movements (and related political parties) in these areas have been changing, and we should not assume for a moment that the past and present patterns will necessarily continue in the future. Thus far such movements and parties have usually been grouped around one person, with only a minimum of lasting ideological or programmatic content present in any one group. Partly under the influence of Marxist ideology and communist organization methods, this is slowly beginning to change.

Likewise, it is at least possible that the strong propensity toward a one-party rule (with sham elections in which everyone excluded from power understandably becomes a bad loser) will become less pronounced than it has been thus far. Possibly the pattern of Mexico and India of actual one-party domination under which other parties are not illegal will make some headway elsewhere. The examples of Japan, Venezuela, and Israel show that a one-party monopoly is certainly not essential to modernization.

Ideological eclecticism, often coupled with phraseological imitation of either Western or Eastern political concepts, has been frequent in modernizing areas and has tended to obscure the actual qualitative differences. The main differences have been: first, the typical lack of a permanent organizational basis for such terminologies and, second, the volatility of organization and the abrupt changes in ideological orientation that characterize social reform movements and political parties in modernizing areas, resulting in frequent splits within each kind of grouping.

On the other hand, the effects of such volatility and propensity to split have not always been unfavorable. The extensive regrouping of reform ideas and organizations led in some cases to a metamorphosis that encouraged the emergence of democratic attitudes and action methods where they were dubious or nonexistent. The transformation of APRA in Peru has not been due just to the aging of Haya de la Torre; the violent APRA of forty years ago has become a mild, almost conservative movement, not only as a result of its long wanderings in a political wilderness, but also as a result of the incipient modernization of the urban-industrial sector and even a fraction of the agrarian sector of Peruvian society.[12] Betancourt's *Acción Democrática* in Venezuela also changed its complexion and action methods very substantially between his two presidencies. Likewise, the left-of-center movement and subsequent regime of the Christian Democrats in Chile was a far cry from the ideology and methods of its predecessors. It is less easy to find comparable examples outside Latin America with its relatively long background of political independence but the point is that the conspicuous propensity for rapid changes in social reform movements in the modernizing areas does not necessarily have adverse effects upon economic society.

It is true that there are examples of unfinished socio-economic revolutions, such as that of Mexico after half a century, or even of degenerated revolutions, such as that of Bolivia under the Nationalist Revolutionary Movement (MNR) after only one decade. But the only thing this proves is that the achievement of actual power by a social reform movement does not mean that the nation will live happily ever after, and that such initial achievement marks a new departure rather than the definitive fulfillment of national aims.

The respective roles of violence and persuasion, and the forms of action and organization in general, appear to differ considerably according to the *phase* of modernization. We should not look for any strict correlation, but the minimum of permanent organization and ideology along with the maximum of violence and volatility are usually to be found in societies that are in very early stages of socio-economic transformation. We are not, of course, referring to stagnating societies of a primitive or feudal type which are not modernizing yet. It is not the incipient but the somewhat more advanced phase of recent modernization that appears to promise more stable organizational forms and action methods in social reform movements and in the actual regimes which they may

40

establish, including greater appeal to persuasion, based in part on progress in mass education. But even there relapses are frequent, especially as this process brings the inclusion into social movements and political life of socio-economic, cultural, and regional subgroups which have had no previous experience of any real participation in national life.

This leaves the question of to what extent the various types of social reform groupings in modernizing areas, which have been discussed in the preceding sections, represent movements in the sense of essentially self-propelling mass actions. It has been shown that their organizational coherence is usually weak and that their action methods and ideologies are volatile. Moreover, we have seen that some of the mass groupings and actions under discussion actually represent movements from above, especially in an authoritarian regime, and that others are mainly noisy clamor from small (for example, intellectual) minority elites. Yet all these reservations should not obscure the fact that there are strong and genuine currents for social reform in nearly all the modernizing areas.

Five conceptual conclusions

First, one aspect of the preceding discussion raises questions on the extent to which the European — North American concepts of economic system fit the conditions of modernizing areas. In fact, these concepts look quite ripe for fundamental re-examination in the developed economies as well; this facet of the problem will be discussed in chapter 7. At any rate, even if we assume that these concepts have, at least, retained *some* value as analytic abstractions in developed areas, their uses in exploring the institutions, attitudes, and aspirations of social movements in the modernizing areas are quite narrow, if we disregard the level of purely phraseological emulation. Above all, private or public ownership is even less of a useful yardstick there than it is in the developed countries of our period.

Second, movements for social reform in modernizing areas are both much broader and much more vague in scope than a quest for another economic system. They are broader in aiming at an overall transformation of socio-economic, cultural, educational, and political conditions, and they are more vague in that they usually have only hazy notions of the specific goal and the best method of attaining it. The *Idealtypus* approach to, say, free enterprise versus collectivism helps them very little in obtaining greater clarity either in their goals and methods or in daily decisions on development policy.

Third, these movements essentially represent a quest for modernization of economic society *and* a protest against early socio-economic effects of such modernization, a protest which varies in its forms and means of expression but is nearly always rooted in the very nature of the innovations achieved.[13] The ideological and political confrontation over these forms and means at times overlaps, but is by no means identical with, a competition between alternative economic systems. More specifically, the almost universally professed socialism of social movements in modernizing areas is usually considered quite compatible with much leeway for private owne p of the means of production, and the real fight is about the best method and leadership in implementing such a development-oriented socialism.

Fourth, the expectation of consistent Western-type rationality on the part of social reform movements in modernizing societies would be unrealistic, even if rational socio-economic or political behavior in the West itself were far more predominant than it has ever been. At the very least, the West needs to understand that the movements just mentioned have their own historical heritage, conceptual framework, and perceived rationality which are by no means identical with those of the West. They may also have quite an elaborate pattern of socio-historical rationalizations, especially those focused on collective villains who are supposed to have prevented their socio-economic progress in the past. Under these conditions, it must be understood that violent, even destructive forms of social protest, while highly undesirable and wasteful, represent an almost inevitable phase of such movements before they and the economic society they reflect reach the subsequent stage of constructive reform.

Fifth, the insight that development of necessity constitutes a far more extensive and complex transformation of society than the rise of per capita income or life expectancy — however important these changes may be as such — has been rapidly, if perhaps not sufficiently, growing both in the underdeveloped and in the developed nations. What now needs to be explored far more thoroughly than before is the question of whether what we classify as development or modernization does not represent a continuous emergence of new socio-economic models of various kinds that are not easily included in the time-honored Western generalizations. Only if we restate the problem in this way shall we be able to grasp the nature of social reform movements in modernizing areas, especially the character of their development-orientation, with its incipient focus on systematic human development no less than on growing availability and utilization of economic resources. We also need to explore more fully the question whether the process of modernization itself does not represent, among other things, a socio-economic system of sorts, whether or not any such relationship applies equally to all the types of modernizing societies, and whether the industrialized nations, particularly the United States, have shown any real understanding toward the social changes and movements in modernizing areas.

Social Reform Movements and Socio-National Identity:
A Scheme of Interrelationships

CHAPTER 3

The Psycho-Cultural Roots of America's International Behavior

Why is the most powerful and wealthy nation in history always involved in one international crisis after another? Why is it (or why does it feel) resented by the world, by allies and foes alike? Is it just *because* it is powerful and wealthy in a world of poverty and underdevelopment, or are there deeper reasons?

The author of this book has long been a citizen of the United States. However, the analysis that follows could not have been written were he not a European by birth and had he not spent several years of his life in Latin America. By no means should this analysis be interpreted as anti-American; it represents a somewhat desperate attempt to help save the many valuable aspects of the American experience for a world of old and new nations, which are impatient for some kind of modernization.

It is the essence of this analysis that the major troubles of America as a nation have been caused by certain basic shortcomings in its ability to understand the thinking, feeling, history, and values of other nations. This lack of understanding, in turn, has reflected the mental block that America has against understanding itself. The dangerous combination of these two limitations has resulted in an unprecedented pattern of semi-conscious double life. The nation that likes to think of itself as the incorporation of realism has entangled itself in a perception of itself and the world in which any resemblance to reality has been purely coincidental.

This interpretation will be traced through the specific characteristics of the mental wall toward others and oneself, the upbringing and role of children in American society with the resulting problems of individualism versus conformity, the roots of mass fears in such a powerful nation, the patterns of black-and-white thinking, a self-view as moral preceptor for the world, the contrast between professed Christian values and widespread acquisitive compulsions, the theory and practice of Free Enterprise, and the habit of appraising all social and international values in terms of money. Some conclusions on the future of America's role in the contemporary world wind up this discussion.

Mental Walls

The most conspicuous weakness of Americans as a nation in their dealings with the outside world has been their almost incredible difficulty in understanding other people. To some extent, of course, they share this difficulty with various other nations, but with Americans it is more sweeping and, at the same time, less conscious in their own minds. They tend to take it for granted that they do understand others, or else that there is really nothing special to understand since people are basically alike everywhere. Before going into the various manifestations and effects of this lack of understanding, it is worthwhile to get at the roots of this limitation, although a systematic cultural and historical analysis of the American way of thinking must be left to specialists in this field. [1]

When America broke loose from colonial domination, and long thereafter, it was faced with the necessity of establishing its national identity. A good many nations are struggling with this task in our own period, as has been shown in Chapter 2. Today, the two prevailing modes of acquiring national identity are socioeconomic development plans or ambitious neoimperialist designs for empire building at the expense of others, or a combination of both.

In the case of the new America some two hundred years ago, neither one of these procedures was necessary or appropriate. The Louisiana Purchase, the Mexican war, and the Alaska deal expanded United States territory enormously without any clear-cut empire-building ambitions being evident. More important than this, the westward drive across the Great Plains and Rocky Mountains to the West Coast offered, until the late nineteenth century, an opportunity for economic and political expansion, which far

46

overshadowed any of the methods of national self-assertion that newly developing nations use now.

Instead, the new America resorted to quite a different device without being entirely conscious of it. In order to establish its identity, it shut itself off mentally from Europe, where most of its settlers had come from, and implicitly from the rest of the world. The formidable geographic barrier of the two oceans came to be matched by a self-imposed mental barrier of an equally forbidding nature. The psychological fight against King George III was to continue for many decades, even centuries, after achieving political independence. It will be shown later to what extent the continuing fight of the businessman and some other socio-economic groups against The Government is still influenced by this mental legacy from colonial days. At the moment, we are more concerned with the thoroughness of America's early attempt to achieve national identity not only by trying to shut itself off politically from the outside world, but by virtually refusing to believe that there *was* an outside world worth knowing, let alone analyzing. To whatever extent there was a world different from America, it seemed obsolete and doomed. Since people were essentially all alike, it was far better to study them in the New World than in the Old.

The continuing effects of this endeavor to achieve national identity through mental isolation have been very far reaching. Understanding them is essential for a grasp of the current relationship between the United States and the rest of the world. This applies most of all to United States' attitudes toward the modernizing nations and toward the revolutionary implications of their growing quest for fundamental social changes. Even when such revolutionary transformation is led by *non*communist forces, as it often is, one likely effect these days is anti-Americanism, simply because America is seen as lacking in sympathy and understanding toward their ways of thinking and goals of social action, and as the bulwark of anti-revolutionary forces everywhere.

In general terms, many Americans have difficulty in realizing that the rest of the world is *not* populated by Americans or even potential Americans, that other people in the world are *not* almost just like themselves, and that most of them are not only *not* like Americans but do not even want to be.[2] The average American has no doubt that all the other nations could, and should, learn a great deal from his country; but he has quite a block against seeing how much the United States could in turn learn from others, from their historical experiences, their values, and in some cases even their technology. The basic difficulty in perceiving such relationships partly explains the fact that so few Americans are successful in learning foreign languages well: the psychological reason is that they do not *really* see why anyone should speak a language other than American.

Another example of this mental wall is the reaction of most American tourists, and many American residents of foreign countries, to their environment. Both groups have a singular capacity — *sometimes* reinforced by conscious action of influential individuals, diplomats, or business companies — to live outside the population that surrounds them, and to "overlook" it. They look for things that are different only in the sense of their being exotic or quaint; aside from this stimulus, they seek the closest possible approximation to American ways, for example, in hotel facilities or entertainment. Curiosity is by no means the same as understanding or even a genuine attempt to achieve it. Here again, such limitations are certainly not confined to Americans but are more drastic and widespread among them than among other visitors to foreign countries.

Even more serious, in a sense, has been the frequent failure of Americans to realize that their own solutions, no matter how effective in their own country, are not always suitable for other people, especially those in modernizing areas. This is exemplified by the persistence of American management consultants and instructors in equating American organizational experience in production, marketing, or industrial relations with the needs of "sound" management anywhere, as if the illiterate peasant somewhere in Indonesia were an American consumer, the semi-Indian laborer in a Peruvian mill an American industrial worker, or the semi-feudal landowner recently gone into manufacturing an American corporation executive. Another example is the monetary policy of such international organisms as the International Monetary Fund, which has been guided mostly by America. This policy has tended to be more orthodox for the modernizing nations than for the United States itself where actual economic policy quite often deviates from wishful norms, as will be shown later.

The basic difficulty in understanding the variety of cultural values, ways of life, and socio-economic needs in the world leads to a strong tendency to regard American experiences or ways of thinking as the only ones that make sense or that are rational. These experiences and ways of thinking become "human nature," which is thought to be competitive, money-minded, and every-

48

thing else that corresponds to the image which Americans have of themselves. This image, indeed, tends to be just as unrealistic as their view of other people.

The root of the difficulty for Americans in perceiving the outside world realistically is their lack of a dependable *medium comparationis* or frame of reference. The America they are taught to see from early childhood represents a wishful image, rather than a faithful reflection of their real country and society. Their training conditions them, often irreparably, to confuse the image of an idealized America which they *wish* to exist with the actual state of affairs in their national environment.[3] This has led to a mental condition of unresolved (and unrealized) contradictions which have been precariously "resolved" through a peculiar pattern of self-brainwashing on such matters as race, communism, and social reform movements in modernizing areas.

On the racial issue, America kept persuading itself until the middle of the twentieth century that previous practices somehow did not violate the principles of freedom and equality that were proclaimed in the Constitution of 1787. Contradictions between principle and practice, in terms both of constitutional philosophy and Christian values, were rationalized away until they *seemed* to be resolved to the satisfaction of the individual and his society. The price which both of them have been paying for this self-imposed mental block will be discussed later, as will the United States' handling of communist threats in the world and of social reform movements in modernizing areas. First, however, we need to analyze the roots of the national self-image of many Americans.

The original immigration, and much of the later, consisted largely of people who were at odds with the institutions, traditions, or prevailing values of their homelands. Many of them were rejecting social conditions such as exploitation, poverty, and religious or political oppression. The immigration from Africa was, of course, altogether involuntary. The original European immigration mainly consisted of young people who wanted to start a new life, to forget the old world with its rigid authoritarian structure of society, and to assert their individual and collective independence. Consciously or not, they imbued their children with these values; but they could not help facing the fact that they themselves had come from that European environment in which their children had no interest. In such cases, Father sometimes became the symbol of the undesirable Old World, and antipaternal attitudes resulted. The (often native-born) Mother, on the other hand, became the protector of the children, and America became "Mother Land." The contrast between the children's relationships to father and mother became a source of unresolved contradictions in the American soul, especially of an unrealistic self-perception. In Erikson's words, "self-contradictions in American history may expose her youth to an emotional and political short-circuit and thus endanger her dynamic potential." [4]

For these reasons, Freud's discussion of the typical domineering father has never quite applied to America, least of all in the twentieth century. The origin of the nation in a revolt against royal authority had led to a fixation upon resistance to authority in general and parental authority in particular. The child, therefore, has been assumed to be well within his right in doing whatever he pleases. The child psychologists and psychoanalysts are believed by many to have proved that any parental attempt at childhood discipline (in extreme cases of misinterpretation, any active attempt at "socialization" of the children) would arouse in the children severe inferiority complexes with a corresponding overcompensation which would bedevil them in their future lives. [5]

To this must be added still another source of the "sacred cow" attitude toward children that has become so widespread in America. By consistently letting them do as they please, the parents expect to condition them for individualism, competition, resourcefulness, even ruthlessness, thus getting them ready for their future adult life in a market economy. This part of the American child-rearing patterns has older historical roots than the pseudo-Freudianism just mentioned. We shall see later how such individual beliefs have affected the collective assumptions of the United States regarding its foreign-policy goals and methods. The cult of youth is further bolstered by associating America itself — now almost 200 years old as a nation — with youth, which is then used as an explanation of, or excuse for, immature behavior, not only on the individual but on the national level.

One aspect of this national descent to the child level of perception and behavior is lack of mature time perspective; a natural phenomenon in children everywhere, but a rare one among adults in economically advanced societies. [6] The inability to foresee the long-range consequences of one's actions or to see that such consequences do matter, assuming that the past is not worth remembering and that everyone should let bygones be bygones, impatience with people, like Europeans and Latin Americans, who keep harping on what happened long ago: these are all characteristics of U.S.

50

foreign policy, which have got it into trouble time and again. How could anyone with a longer vision than a child's have lined up U.S. power time and again on the side of doomed, semi-feudal land-owning classes and brutal dictatorships, while theoretically claiming the principles of freedom and democracy?

What sometimes looks like the subtlety of a bull in a china shop is actually part of a self-imposed, semi-conscious regression of national and governmental thinking to the child level of illusions of omnipotence; it is living in the present oblivious to the past, and lacking vision of the future. We shall further discuss the pattern of U.S. foreign relations in a later section. Before that we need to explore a number of basic contradictions among American values and practices.

Individualism and Conformity

From a very early age the American child is typically imbued with the importance of achieving "success," largely in the sense of the possession of material goods. He is to do so competitively, at the expense of others, if necessary. Everybody, regardless of class origin, who wants to "succeed" supposedly can do so. If he does not, it is his own fault, not that of social circumstances. Since everybody is assumed to have this chance to succeed, the one who fails to do so will feel utterly discouraged with himself. This is in contrast to his European or Asian brother who is usually quite pleased with, or at least resigned to, his humble station in life, simply because he has never perceived an alternative.

Mailer sums up the attitude of a group of young Americans as follows, "If they all stuck together -- all they knew was to cut each other's throats."[7] They all had been conditioned to a *bellum omnium contra omnes*. The roots of this attitude can probably be traced again to a fixation of the anti-authoritarian fight against colonial rule, reinforced by the influence and reinterpretation of early capitalistic competition in Great Britain, and by the culturally conditioned attempt in America to constantly prove one's manliness in an essentially matriarchal society.

American children tend to interpret the family as revolving about themselves, and happiness as getting or having something material , while children in many other cultures see work, education, and obligations to their parents as the major aspects of life. In various cultures children assume paternal authority to be life-long, in contrast to American parents who are afraid to displease their children.[8] Now the peculiar thing about this child-centered and individualistic-materialistic culture is that *everybody* is expected to strive for individual success in about the same way, even though obviously everybody cannot come out on top. Moreover, only the person who behaves in a certain *collectively established* manner can hope to achieve individual success; otherwise all the other individualists will collectively gang up on him and make his success impossible.

One must understand this strange combination of individualism along with rather rigid collective standards for its actual enactment — a self-understanding which is not very widespread — in order to grasp the full range in American life of the built-in contradiction between constant and usually sincere assertions of unprecedented individual freedom and the constant pressure for conformity sometimes approaching totalitarian forms. The contradiction is "resolved" by expecting everybody to arrive individually at the same standard conclusions and opinions. To restate the point, conformity is internalized here to such an extent that each American honestly believes that he has arrived at his ideas and behavior in a strictly individual way. He merely expects every other person to arrive at exactly the same ideas and behavior in *his* "individual" way.

On the *abstract* level, needless to say, Americanism has always assumed that individualism was sacred. No human being, leader, political group, or social movement has been deemed omniscient enough to monopolize all the wisdom and to be guaranteed exclusive power. Free Americans were to be able to decide, both during and between elections, whether it was time for a change in policies or not, and free competition of ideas was to be the basis of such decisions. The person who disagreed with you, with the President, or with the Supreme Court was assumed to be well within his rights and to be subjectively as sincere and well-intentioned as those he disagreed with. Constant debate among the holders of many diverging opinions and ideologies was seen as the most valuable asset of Americanism.

Yet, the *practice* of American life has been rather different, and this is no less true now than it had been earlier. The Alien and Sedition Act, the Know Nothing movement, the Palmer raids, the Ku Klux Klan, the House Committee on Un-American Activities, and McCarthyism mark only a few phases of the witch hunts against "dangerous thought," which have been a recurrent trend in the life of the nation. Not surprisingly, they have in each case been presented as legitimate and necessary in order to preserve American freedom against some kind of villain — the French, the Communists, or whoever. In each case many thousands of people saw no contradiction involved in throwing freedoms away in order to supposedly preserve freedom.

External threats or failures stimulated or helped rationalize, but by no means explain, this propensity for witch-hunting. It is true that external troubles, the latest of which has been the Vietnam trauma, have periodically shaken the collective youngster out of his childhood dreams of omnipotence.

"Americans advertise themselves as 'masters of their own fate.' Concretely this means that Americans tend to blame only themselves for their frustrations and that they incline to be self-aggressive when they fail."[9] In genuine totalitarian societies, the blame is usually put on out-groups (e.g. in Nazi Germany on the Allies of the First World War and then on the "international Jew"); in a society torn by *contradictions* between democratic ideology and totalitarian activities, the blame for setbacks abroad is easily channeled toward domestic "traitors." The belief that the United States "lost" China — as if it had ever owned it — helped unleash Joseph McCarthy's great chase after those in the United States who were to blame.

Perhaps the most conspicuous characteristic of totalitarian currents in the United States, as elsewhere, is anti-intellectualism. Children are not intellectually minded, and a society which makes adults defer to children can clearly have nothing but resentful contempt for "eggheads." This plays admirably into the hands of genuine totalitarians who hate nothing more than a challenge to their blind destructive emotions. Totalitarian mentality, to be sure, is an extreme form of the more widespread tendencies in the United States toward a standardized conformity, which is in contradiction with the individualistic values glorified on the overt level. In fact, such standardization, along with a repression of divergent individual needs, may account in some degree for the high incidence of certain mental disorders. Constant fear of unintended nonconformity haunts the "individualist," while successful conformity may give him some feeling of security.

The root of the amazing fearfulness of Americans as a cultural group (of which they are only partly aware) appears to be a fixation of the typical insecurity feelings of the adolescent who is unable to get his bearings in a highly complex world and is engaged in a desperate search for identity. Ordinarily such immaturity in the life of an individual adolescent is a passing phase in his personality development. But it can in some cases lead to a fixation for life; such a person is unable to outgrow his immaturity ever. It is far more surprising to see analogous cases in the life of a nation, especially a rich and powerful one. David Riesman's famous classification of Americans as The Lonely Crowd is more descriptive of this situation than even he realized, in the most literal sense.

This mechanism of fear and distrust, often expressed in group hatreds, is dealt with mainly in two ways: first, through boastfulness and, second, through a frantic endeavor to be loved by other people, in the outside world — without, indeed, making a corresponding attempt to love or even to understand the others, as was shown earlier. Nations that are reasonably self-assured and feel that they have defined their identity — say, the British — do not try to find out all the time what others think of them; more likely, they care little about it, at least as long as it does not affect specific interests and decisions of a political or economic nature. Americans, on the other hand, are bewildered and hurt when the Cambodians or the Italians or the Mexicans, or even the Russians, do not love them. Since most Americans like to hear all the time from others, as well as from themselves, how wonderful they are, they are extremely touchy when a foreigner, or even a naturalized American with a foreign accent, gently implies that America might be somewhat less than perfect — even when the native American who listens has just said far more critical things about his country himself.

When things at home or abroad do not seem to go quite the way they should, or when the contradiction between bombastic language and deep fears becomes too conspicuous, the problem is temporarily resolved by an outbreak of mass hysteria, channeled and organized by some committee of investigation or an extra-parliamentary vigilante group.[10] The whole population then becomes a refugee of sorts, trying to escape from real problems and too complex a reality, looking desperately for scapegoats and easy answers. Needless to say, more frustrations result from such organized mass hysteria, and some day the fad changes and the pendulum begins to swing back — or so it has *thus far* each time — after many persons have been victimized. But is there any guarantee that it will always swing back in the future, and how many such waves can even a rich and powerful nation afford without destroying itself?

Black-and-White Thinking

It is fearfulness, more than any other influence, which makes it difficult for so many Americans to understand complexities and delays in international, ideological, and sometimes in national affairs.[11] If one is constantly afraid that others are conspiring against him and that the next moment may be the last unless he acts quickly, he will not be in a mood for analytic study of the situation, long-range consideration of all the factors involved, or diplomatic and psychological subtleties. (This is where the typical American fears in world affairs differ from the Russian which, for different historical and psychological reasons, can also approach a paranoid condition without, however, as a rule, dispensing with shrewd calculation, subtle timing, and the long view.) It has been pointed out earlier that the regression of adult thinking processes to the child level, also precludes intricate consideration of long-range factors.

It is a moot question whether the resulting attitude toward international and domestic problems has been shaped by "Western" movies or whether it has merely resulted in their everlasting popularity. In all probability there has been an interaction, but it is amazing to observe time and again how closely United States behavior in world affairs, in particular, has followed the pattern of the Westerns. There are good guys and bad guys — no other guys. The extent to which United States foreign policy has followed this pattern of assumptions, under both Republican and Democratic administrations, will surely astonish future historians. The good guy, *of course*, is the United States at all times; the bad guy in the last 25 years or so has been the communist powers, although the splitting up of the monolith into Russian, Chinese, Yugoslav, Cuban, and other sectors has made simplification a good deal more difficult. At any rate, the United States has classified the world's regimes into two categories. One category consists of the communist nations without too much regard to the variations mentioned, and a constant tendency to appoint as "honorary" Communists all those whose policies the United States does not like at the moment or who have had the temerity to be critical of some United States actions. The other category is called The Free World and includes everybody and anybody who is not communistic: Franco, Salazar, Trujillo, Syngman Rhee, Emperor Haile Selassie, King Saud or Feisal, Chiang Kai-shek. If Hitler and Mussolini were still around, their regimes would today presumably be classified as part of The Free World, for they were anti-communist, were they not? The Cuban case has been the most absurd of all, although its Dominican aftermath showed how little the United States had learned from the Cuban experience. Most people familiar with Cuban history will agree that without past United States support for the Batista tyranny, there would in all probability be no *fidelismo* today. For years, the United States supported Batista politically, financially, and militarily; his officers and troops were American-trained and American-equipped. Batista and his officials were easy to do business with and to buy; United States free enterprise knew their price. Moreover, they seemed to be a bulwark of The Free World against communism, even though the Communist Party was actually on fairly good terms with them much of the time, in fact until the very eve of Castro's breaking out of the Sierra Maestra. He then defeated with his handful of guerrillas the heavily armed, United States trained forces of the regime. Since the U.S. had supported Batista, what could the victorious rebels be expected to be but anti-United States? The reason, at first, was not that they were Communists; they went communist (absorbing and replacing the old Communist Party) because they had been made anti-United States largely by this country's own actions.

Then came the Bay of Pigs disaster, due to reports by intelligence agents who knew everything and understood nothing. President Kennedy's handling of the subsequent blockade crisis in the fall of 1962 showed that the United States *could* understand foreign policy and diplomacy. But this was followed in 1965 by an acute relapse into the old mentality, in the Dominican affair. The good guys had been told that the bad guys were about to take over that country; the good guys pulled the trigger first and all of them lived happily thereafter — or did they? By invading another country, without notifying the O.A.S. or the U.N. of the crisis as formal commitments required, the U.S. — which, of course, had a history of military occupations of the Dominican Republic and other Caribbean countries — created countless communists all over Latin America while trying to get rid of the actual or imaginary ones in the Dominican Republic the way that the time-honored pattern of the "Westerns" prescribed.

The United States had once more failed to understand that ideas, no matter how obnoxious, cannot successfully be fought by either guns or money. Irrational fear, which in the fifties and sixties happened to be focused on communism, had played into the hands of the real communist powers by pushing U.S. policy once more into the blundering which comes from insensitivity nourished by irrational fears. This mentality had also made the U.S. once more an object of contempt and pity in a large part of the world and had aroused strong nationalist resentment all over Latin America. Recently, the most tragic example of such perceptual limitations has of course, been the Vietnam affair. There is no need to add here to the already voluminous books, articles, and speeches on this subject, except to point out that Vietnam has brought out on a large scale all the characteristics of American thinking that have been discussed earlier. These include the belief that the United States must and can have its way at all times, the fear-ridden Domino Theory, the belief that ideologies, military superiority, and the affection of other nations can all be bought for cash, the persistent self-deception practises employed by the Government and long accepted by millions of people.[1][2] We may add the basic inability to understand the reactions of millions of Vietnamese, both in the North and the South, toward the foreign devils who had invaded and corrupted their country, even though they supposedly only wanted to rid it from that domestic devil, communism. The U.S. took it for granted that the Vietnamese, just like themselves, would primarily want to avoid pain and destruction and that they could, therefore, be bombed into yielding and surrendering. But the Vietnamese, like many other Asians, had been conditioned for ages to work, to learn, to please their parents, and if necessary to suffer and to die. They reacted to escalation in an "unreasonable" manner according to *American* standards, namely by taking any amount of punishment and responding to escalation by counter-escalation regardless of cost.

The cultural misunderstanding cost the U.S. dearly. It remains to be seen whether the traumatic experience in Vietnam marks the end of moralism and self-deception in America, or whether the psychological effects of this war will fizzle out in a general atmosphere of uneasiness, apprehension, fatigue, mutual reproaches, and violence.

So much is certain, that the Vietnam trauma, especially the "credibility gap," has shaken a substantial proportion of the college population out of the apathy of yesterday and into a rebellion against the perceived sickness of society and its pseudo-rational righteousness. The rebels consider themselves to be revolutionaries, radicals, sometimes anarchists, but in reality, many of them have little in common with any of these. Even the anarchists, and more so the Marxists, have always wanted to tear down the existing society in order to replace it by a better one of which they had a blueprint. The pseudo-revolutionaries and pseudo-radicals of recent years have been driven by essentially negative, often destructive urges and have not been interested in constructive alternatives. Basically, they are merely acting out delayed emotional, often authoritarian, needs from childhood and adolescence, needs which normally disappear in the course of growing-up but have undergone in these cases a fixation that has made them continue into adulthood. There certainly is plenty to complain about and to improve in the universities and in society, but any resemblance between rational demands and the excited noises made by the destructive fringe has been purely coincidental.

In order to grasp more fully the international effects of the social dislocation in America, we will now discuss the place of moralism in these effects. Among the great semi-conscious contradictions that characterize contemporary American culture, one of the most conspicuous is the contrast between the dog-eats-dog philosophy, and the belief that there is one pattern of morality — represented by the United States — which is entitled and destined to dominate world affairs. What most foreign observers have great difficulty in understanding is the fact that this moralism is on the whole *subjectively* honest, not hypocritical. Many Americans really believe that their nation holds the key to what is right in and for the world, even though, through an extraordinary coincidence, this always turns out to be identical with U.S. foreign policy aims. Most Americans genuinely believe in their national superiority over other people, not only economically but morally.[13] In fact, they associate these two things, in the Puritan tradition.

The inevitable reasoning that follows then implies that most other people, if not outright savages, at least need to be taught about the dangers of communism of which, in their intellectual or moral weakness, they may not be sufficiently aware. Once they have been properly instructed and civilized they will readily follow the U.S. lead and will, in particular, stop criticizing America. The thought that such criticism just *might* result from the U.S. having done something wrong is alien to the prevailing American thinking.

The otherwise assumed virtues of competition are not deemed to apply to world affairs, even though Soviet Russia, and communism in general, have by now actually beaten America at its own "missionary" game in some modernizing countries. There is

58

only one legitimate policeman and missionary, combined in one country, for the whole world, and nobody should question his principles or action.[14] What has been called the illusion of American omnipotence is based on definite moral convictions as well as a superficial cultural optimism. Since moral right is always assumed to be on the side of the U.S., problems arising in world affairs must be "solved" without delay; it is not enough to live with them as comfortably as possible; problems that do not fit into established preconceptions and self-deceptions must be re-interpreted until they conform to them. For example what James Reston has called "a conflict between power and faith" makes it extremely difficult for Congress and many people to grasp the fact that there is not, and probably never will be, an effective antiballistic missile system to prevent nuclear destruction of major cities. For the same psychological reason, tactical retreats in world affairs are impossible or, at least, must be carefully concealed from political critics, the public, and the press. This is by no means easy since people with teen-age mentality must constantly brag *in advance* about all the magnificent achievements — technological, political, or military — which they are going to accomplish.[15] Moreover, why should anyone retreat from a lofty moral principle? And is not the press in a competitive society "entitled" to constant leaks, even if they endanger national interest or international peace? Why should anyone wish to delay even for hours the announcement of the latest implementation of international morality?

While the whole world is deemed to be a self-decreed responsibility of the U.S., there is, simultaneously, a tendency to consider each area and aspect of world events separately as it occurs, without allowing for interdependence in space and time. This applies conspicuously to modernization processes. An experienced Brazilian observer speaks of the tendency in the U.S. "to sacrifice sociologic intelligence in favor of a moralistic viewpoint in the evaluation of the phenomenon of underdevelopment. This viewpoint focuses preferentially on the degree of perfection in the discharge of imagined tasks, imposed a priori, and omits from its horizon the politico-social complexity of the underdeveloped world. ... final values are frequently confused with intermediate values — specific short-range objectives are taken as authentic national interests of the United States." [16]

For similar psychological reasons, there were few who readily recognized the roots of the Near Eastern crisis of 1967, especially in Soviet policy there, as being in Vietnam. Such "surprises" in various parts of the world, the brushfires and the make-shift responses to them, are the almost inevitable effect of an unhistorical and atomistic approach to world affairs. Moreover, the detailed conduct of U.S. foreign policy depends in large measure on the pedestrian wish of many politicians to be re-elected over and over again; a wish that is by no means universal in democratic societies. The leaks, tactical rigidities, and moral sermons to the nation and the world are, rightly or wrongly, regarded as essential for such political self-perpetuation. Very practical considerations thus interact with moral principles in a unique and highly ritualized way.

Christian Values and Acquisitive Compulsions

Religion occupies in America an interesting and peculiar role. On the one hand, the Constitution and the prevailing Protestant tradition require a strict separation of State and Church. The idea of a state religion is alien to Americans. But the United States has long had a "civil religion" under which God has been constantly invoked by public figures when taking an official oath, making Presidential statements, or defending policing and missionary actions in various parts of the world. [17]

The most conspicuous contradiction between religion and society exists between the ritualistic, organized parareligiosity with its constant appeals to Christian values, and the acquisitive compulsions in the daily life of American society. [18] The contrast between the religious, anti-materialistic theory underlying American life and the acquisitive compulsiveness in its daily practice is not entirely new in history, nor has it originated in America. [19] The Calvinist and Puritan tradition seemingly resolved it by considering thrift, capital accumulation, and hard work as matters of Christian virtue and calling, which were rewarded by economic success; and this tradition has certainly entered into the contemporary rationalizations through which the contradictions described are "resolved." But there are other, more recent factors in these contradictions, and in order to understand them we must look somewhat more deeply into image and reality in the economic set-up which is usually characterized in popular semantics as Free Enterprise.

Many Americans remain convinced that their's is a land, perhaps *the* land, of Free Enterprise and that it is an important part of their mission in the world to preach to all other nations the advantages and benefits of that system. The modernized version of Free Enterprise, it is true, no longer aims at full laissez-faire. State intervention is now considered legitimate, even necessary, when it aims at *aiding* private enterprise, most often at the expense of the general taxpayer. Intervention for the benefit of the less prosperous socio-economic groups, or for the general purpose of maintaining a healthy economy, is still viewed by many as damaging interference with the laws of the universe, although Keynesian concepts have made a substantial dent in the conservative economic upbringing of the man in the street, and even the business community. But when the Johnson Administration submitted, in 1964, a program for tax reductions designed to bring about a revival of the economy and, thereby an increase in *future* tax revenues, pressure in the Congress and in the public for a corresponding reduction of federal expenditures (which, of course, would have undone the reviving effect of the tax reductions) was still heavy. Conversely, when the Administration pressed, in 1968, for a supposedly anti-inflationary increase in taxes, pressure for a simultaneous reduction in Federal expenditures was *also* heavy, and succeeded. In other words, many spokesmen for Free Enterprise still had not grasped the fiscal (and perhaps the monetary) impact of Keynesian modernization.

The basic mistrust of government, more of the federal government than state or local authorities, remains deeply ingrained in American culture. It was mentioned earlier that this has resulted from a fixation of the fight against colonial rule, in which this nation had its origin; some psychoanalysts see in it a kind of collective father complex, but this is a more doubtful interpretation.[20] The contradiction between this fundamental hostility toward a government which centuries ago supposedly became "We the People" and the constant acceptance and solicitation of government intervention on the practical level remains just as unresolved, and often unrealized or unconscious, as the contradictions discussed earlier; and it has had a similar corroding effect under the surface of American culture. The cleavage between the wishful image of Free Enterprise and the reality of a strongly and permanently interventionist economy continues to bedevil the country's adjustment to the world in the late twentieth century. Many Americans continue to assume that by *calling* the present U.S. economy Free Enterprise, it actually *becomes* Free Enterprise; and they then go out into the world and preach the gospel of it to others as if they had implemented it in their own country.

Moreover, in the conceptual world of the contemporary United States, Free Enterprise is still associated with capitalism. The connotation of capitalism to most Americans still includes a high and steadily rising standard of living for everybody. It is only recently that poverty in America has been "discovered", but it remains to be seen whether the various anti-poverty campaigns will represent more than just another passing fad. Certainly, there is a glaring inconsistency between this "discovery" and the time-honored perception of capitalism as guaranteeing ever greater prosperity and equality.

The contradiction is even more bothersome with regard to the *international* effects of the prevailing belief in capitalism. Americans like to classify either as capitalism or free enterprise every trend in the U.S. which they consider favorable, especially trends toward higher incomes and greater equality in consumption, exaggerated as such beliefs may often be. But Latin Americans, Asians, Africans, and very many Europeans associate the concept of capitalism with the economic and social conditions that Engels and Marx wrote about around the middle of the nineteenth century. Actually, the present condition of peasants and workers in many parts of the world, especially in newly industrializing areas with a feudal legacy, often resembles those conditions to a considerable degree. Few Americans are prepared to draw subtle distinctions between what they call capitalism in their own country and period, and what *other* populations associate with capitalism, past or present, in *their* parts of the world. For these other people, capitalism means exploitation, chronic unemployment, child labor, wages at the barest subsistence level, illiteracy, mass diseases, short life-expectancy, monopolies, lack of social mobility, slums and shantytowns, and foreign economic domination.

The basic reason for the block that many Americans have toward such distinctions, is once again, *fear*. Remove one stone from the conceptual structure of "capitalism" as they have built it up in their own minds and the whole structure will collapse, leaving them mentally in a strange uncharted world. So Americans keep preaching "capitalism" to the rest of the world, thus alienating it, and then they feel hurt and puzzled when the world does not love them and their capitalist Free Enterprise. The two remedies which they tend to apply to such a situation are, first, a show of affluence and, second, public relations techniques. The show of affluence is sometimes effective in other countries but tends to backfire when it is overdone. It is one thing to try to set an example by supplying inexpensive mass consumption goods of acceptable quality; it is quite another to consider such goods the *only* thing that matters to anybody. Worse than that, mass consumption loses much of its attractiveness to others, including many poverty-stricken populations, when it degenerates into the senseless waste which has become an accepted and largely internalized way of life in the U.S.

Other nations, which have experienced for countless generations a tradition of economically motivated thrift or of basic poverty in which waste was considered irresponsible, have little understanding for the antics of an Affluent Society. They sometimes feel morally insulted by the wastefulness of Americans in the midst of other people's abysmal poverty, and are bewildered by the apparent association between capitalism, free enterprise, and wastefulness in American life and values. The bewilderment reaches its peak when waste interacts with the kind of generosity that implies that everything (and everybody) in the world can be bought for money.

Is Everything in the World for Sale?

Among the various contradictions in the American mind and behavior, on which this analysis is focused, the most conspicuous and probably the most damaging to America's standing in the world has been the cleavage between the moralism discussed earlier and the prevailing assumption that everything and everybody in the world can be purchased for money. Above all, the belief has been widespread that other populations are under a kind of moral obligation to love America and Americans, and that the only reason why some of them have not has been that the U.S. has not spent enough money on them.

Ella giammai m'amò, exclaims in painful despair the aging King Philip II of Spain, in Verdi's opera Don Carlo, when he discovers that his young Queen had never loved him, even though he had assumed that it was her moral duty to do so. America, being convinced of its own morality as well as superiority, has always been at a loss to understand why everybody does not love it. The assumption is that whenever there is trouble for the U.S. in the world, the remedy is to appropriate more money. The frequent inability to see any social relationships, especially the relations among nations, in terms other than money-plus-public-relations

63

has done the standing of the U.S. in the world more harm than all the communist propaganda drives put together. The obsession with expressing everything — way of life, economic progress, social attitudes, family relationships, even religion — in quantitative, often pecuniary, terms has often vexed other populations. Thence the paradoxical spectacle of American generosity and its unexpected international effects. On the one hand, there has been some genuine magnanimity and readiness to help; on the other hand, there has been the naive and not very dignified expectation that generosity will pay off, if not literally, then at least by winning a great popularity contest in world affairs.

Nowhere has this deeply rooted belief in *financial* generosity had a greater impact on U.S. actions than in foreign aid policy, especially development aid of a bilateral character. The very concept of "aid" implies unselfish purposes. If the U.S. had given or even loaned money and goods to modernizing nations in a genuine spirit of aiding *them*, the effect on its own standing in the world and on the principles of international policy making in general might have been revolutionary. Instead, U.S. foreign aid policy became just another diplomatic gimmick and was promptly recognized by others as such. The cult of bigness, rather than quality, in programming and staffing made things a good deal worse, but the basic fault lay with the U.S. interpretation of aid itself. If there is trouble somewhere in the world, if things are not going the way you want them to, just appropriate *more* money. If communism raises its head somewhere, just buy off those whom you suspect of wavering.

Aid became a mere financial technique designed to ward off communism. Not surprisingly, it was rarely a successful technique. In a more general vein, aid became a public relations trick, a way of campaigning for votes abroad. Occasionally, aid for potentially revolutionary aims, such as the Alliance for Progress, became a belated act of atonement for earlier support of reactionary landowners and dictators, and in Latin America a desperate attempt to forestall the spread of *fidelismo*. The U.S. has given extensively, but it has given most readily when it has been frightened; and then it has not always given to the right people, in the right manner, or with the right understanding of the cultural values and needs of the recipients. In order to avoid continuous disappointments, the U.S. needs to realize that financial generosity should *supplement* genuine ideas and values, not try to be a substitute for them. The most effective public relations consist in impressive performance

64

at home along with basic humility and understanding abroad. No amount of money or propaganda will cause the world to become more than superficially Americanized.

A Western nation that is to survive must be able to understand international differences among cultures, value systems, social structures, economic and political arrangements, approaches to international relations and, above all, the difference between wishful image and social reality. This lack of understanding has bedeviled U.S. attitudes, first, toward the League of Nations and then, in different ways, toward the United Nations. The U.N. gradually came to count on American generosity not only in financial, but in political crises: U.N. forces were sent to Palestine, Cyprus, and the Congo largely at U.S. insistence and expense. In the cases of Korea and the Dominican Republic, international backing mainly represented window dressing for American actions.

Much could be added on the *domestic* effects of the belief that everything and everybody is for sale. In fact, the international effects just discussed would hardly have happened if this belief were less deeply rooted in American life. Not until Americans as a nation come to recognize more clearly that there are important values and influences in national and international life *other* than money, and take this insight into their own thinking and living habits at home, will they have a reasonable propect of understanding the rest of the world. Not until then can they end the periodic foreign hostility, which they have unwittingly elicited at the highest financial expense in history.

Conclusion

The basic reason why Americans as a nation have had such difficulty in understanding the outside world has been their inability to understand themselves. And the reason for this phenomenon, the lack of a realistic perception of their own society, culture, and process of change, has been the sad and paradoxical fact that they have been blinded by fear.

But does America really depend on constant fearful self-deception both with regard to itself and to the rest of the world? For a great and powerful nation to behave in international relations like a perennial, misunderstood adolescent is not only immature but unrealistic, thus dangerous to itself and to the peace of the world. In the words of Hans J. Morgenthau,

What is so profoundly disturbing in our Vietnam policies is ... that they derive from erroneous conceptions about the nature of foreign policy and from a distorted view of reality... If a foreign policy is based upon a world view which has but a tenuous relation to reality, if the sheerest dilettantism, however confidently practiced, informs a foreign policy, change requires not just a pragmatic adaptation of action to reality but a radical transformation of one's modes of thought and action. Such a transformation requires first of all a moral effort allowing the truth to prevail against persistent error with which the ego of the policy-maker is identified. It is obvious the men who make our foreign policy...tend to identify themselves ever more closely with attitudes, conceptions, and policies which are not only likely to fail on pragmatic grounds but are afflicted with the congenital defects of wrong conceptions and an unrealistic view of the world. [21]

Pseudo-liberals who interpret world events, especially unpleasant ones, in terms of individual or collective villains, rather than deeply rooted cultural traits and other objectively observable factors in society, and who think it the height of progressivism to keep pointing their finger at all the bad things, real or imagined, in national life instead of weighing them against the good ones, only contribute in their own way to the atmosphere of unreality in the domestic and international affairs of the United States.

It will require attitudinal changes of staggering scope and intensity for the United States to rid itself of unrealistic perceptions, at home and abroad. It must resolve the perennial conflict between the thin layer of innocent, optimistic, boastful, sometimes gullible, self-confidence and the deep roots of suspicion and fearfulness; between the overt materialistic-quantitative value system and the desperate inner need for altruistic good deeds; between a moralizing righteousness toward the outside world and a lack of genuine humility or, in Senator Fulbright's term, the arrogance of power; between a burning interest in what others think about America and a desire to be loved by everybody, and touchiness toward those who have the temerity to use a more discriminating approach; and between professed individualism and actual conformity.

This is compounded by unresolved conflicts between the aspiration to missionary conversion of other nations and a fundamental lack of confidence in oneself; between the constant urge for action with immediate results and the necessities of long-range planning in regard to complex world problems; between the wish to be the champion of revolutionary changes in world society and the fearful clinging to forces and institutions from the past; between "manic-depressive" peaks and troughs in the national mood depending on the latest headlines; between outward faith in the power of rational persuasion and a romantic knight-in-shining-armor self-image toward the outside world; between the frequent profession of a supremacy of civilian over military authority and action, and the panicky reliance upon military men and action principles whenever there is a crisis; between the lofty principle of self-determination and freedom for other nations and the requirement that they all conform to *U.S.* ideas of what kind of regime they ought to have and so forth.

Will America soon begin to see itself as it really is, to get away from uncritical self-glorification barely concealing a basic fearful insecurity? Will it stop seeing other nations as if they all really were almost just like America? Will it stop getting upset whenever someone suggests that there can be *many* valid ways of life, socio-economic arrangements, and diplomatic policies? Will it cease resenting or minimizing implicitly all the people in the world who have not become like Americans? Will it reconcile itself to the thought that Americanism is an historical occurrence confined to one part of the world, not an act of will which all the populations of the world should be expected to perform sooner or later?

And if such attitudinal change can be expected to occur in the U.S., will this happen before an unrealistic perception of itself and others, rooted in deep-seated fears, leads it to self-destruction, as has happened to other powerful regimes and civilizations throughout the history of mankind? Time will tell; but these days time is in very short supply. Without such basic changes, the United States will not be able to provide the moral and economic encouragement in international modernization that some two billion people are looking for, nor the effective stimulus so badly needed in establishing a saner world in general.

Before we concentrate once more on the attitudinal problems facing modernizing nations today, we need to look into a specific manifestation of the attitudinal problems of developed countries, business uncertainty and its relationship to industrial development.

CHAPTER 4

Business Uncertainty and
Industrial Development

From the viewpoint of a modernizing nation, the developed countries may look as if they had overcome most of the uncertainties, especially economic ones, that have plagued poverty-stricken populations since time immemorial. In the present chapter we shall examine the question of to what extent any such assumption corresponds to social and psychological reality.

The growing realization in recent years that there is a wide range of psychological, even psychopathological influences on economic action has thrown new light on decision-making in business management, both in economically advanced and in newly modernizing societies. In particular, the concept of uncertainty as applied to business situations has begun to assume new, psychologically more meaningful aspects.

Uncertainty in a *formal* or generalized sense is present as an intrinsic aspect of any situation in which an individual or a group faces future unknown elements, especially when such a situation requires decisions. This is the case regardless of whether uncertainty is defined in terms of the objective conditions of unpredictability or of the subjective perception of such conditions.

Uncertainty concepts in economic literature from Western sources have mostly been of this formal or generalized type, and in most cases of the objective variant. By the use of deductive logic and frequently mathematical generalization, timeless relationships have been formulated, independent of the varying social settings — especially of value systems, stages of development, types of eco-

68

nomic order, class structure, and governmental arrangements. Such formal study has some useful applications but is not the focus of this discussion. By contrast, attention here will be centered on the *substantive* influence of cultural, socio-psychological, historical, and political factors upon the occurrence, spread, and effect of specific perceptions or attitudes of uncertainty that may influence business behavior.

In considering managerial action in industrialized countries during recent decades, the following interrelated categories of substantive uncertainties suggest themselves: (1) unpredictabilities in the economic parameters of action of the firm, in either the long run or the short run; (2) uncertainties concerning political or international developments; (3) uncertainties with respect to the status of the individual in the firm and, at the same time, to the role of the businessman in society; (4) uncertainties or conflict situations with regard to the goals of decision-making and the responsibilities of management. The impact of uncertainty on business behavior could not be studied adequately if one confined oneself to looking at the first type only, important as it is. We need to examine the other three types, as well.

In this particular discussion, the first category will be largely ignored, and little attention will be paid to short-term social and political factors in business uncertainty or to immediate reactions to change in the daily conduct of business. Attention will be centered primarily on long-range uncertainties, of the third and fourth types, that develop and change simultaneously for sizable numbers of firms in an industrialized society and that may affect decision-making and business behavior over extended periods. We must also consider the institutionalization of some types of expectations, a process that limits some kinds of uncertainties.

Uncertainty and Perception Patterns

Subjective uncertainty in the sense used here is an attitude or state of mind involving a feeling of incomplete knowledge or control of conditions relevant to decision-making. Thus business uncertainty, like other uncertainties, reflects one kind of perception — in this case, the predominant perception managers have of economic (or other) happenings and trends that they interpret as inconclusive. This interpretation may or may not be realistic, or objectively justified, but it will affect business behavior. It may lead to deferred decisions, to looking in the files for precedents, to a search for further information, or to other results, but in any case, it will be influential in shaping business action, or inaction.

Uncertainty as a subjective attitude is to be clearly distinguished from "objective uncertainties," i.e., from unpredictable (or imperfectly predictable) conditions. Objective uncertainty defined narrowly may be said to exist *outside* the decision-maker; it is definable in relation to *any* decision-maker. Examples of such objectively uncertain eventualities are: future prices when they are beyond the control of the decision-maker; action by a new labor union which may seek to assert its existence through a demonstrative strike; the interpretation of antitrust laws by the courts with respect to an unprecedented business policy. The kinds of social factors influencing these objective uncertainties are: the types and amounts of *intrinsically* unpredictable change that is inherent in the social order; and the extent and spread of information concerning future eventualities that are in principle predictable. In many situations, a manager will be able to adjust to incomplete knowledge sufficiently for purposes of action. In extreme situations action may be paralyzed.

However, what is *perceived* as uncertainty, and its effects on action, will depend not only on objective conditions but also on: (1) the general attitudinal environment in the society or the business population, e.g., the value placed on security versus progress; (2) the presence or absence of institutionalized solutions of action problems in the face of given kinds of objective unpredictabilities; and (3) the individual's psychological make-up. The first and second of these conditions, the first in particular, will recur in various contexts throughout this discussion. Here a brief comment on individual differences must suffice. Some individuals may underrate objective uncertainties, tending to underestimate the potentialities of change and its unpredictability. Some who assess the objective factors realistically may nevertheless enjoy a gamble. In still other cases, uncertainty perceptions may be exaggerated as a result of strong personal insecurity which blurs a person's vision or makes him incapable of reaching decisions. Subjective insecurity may thus be a causative factor in unrealistic perceptions of uncertainty, and the process may be cumulative if feelings of insecurity are increased further by failure to resolve uncertainties.

Perceptions of uncertainty and indecisiveness are not the same thing, though there may be a high correlation between the two. Nor should insecurity and uncertainty be confused. Subjective uncertainty refers to a perceived lack of conclusiveness in a situation; insecurity refers to a perceived threat in the social environment or, at least, lack of assurance in a person. I have discussed elsewhere the relationship between socio-economic instability and the incidence of personal insecurities.[1] The same socio-economic instabilities that are related to some types of personal insecurity may also impede the formation of definite long-term expectations by individuals in various spheres of life, including business. This will depend in part on the cultural environment in which business is conducted in a given case.

Culture, Socio-Historical Setting, and Uncertainty

The culture of a population expresses a system of basic values that profoundly colors its perception of the world, of itself, and of the aims of economic activity. Culture, broadly defined, also includes lasting social organization and patterns of group interaction. Thus in many ways, culture affects the quality and intensity of uncertainty feelings that are of a long-range type, especially those relating to social status, roles, and goals. Culture likewise shapes the prevailing time perspective, that is, the extent to which individuals typically think ahead and decide ahead. This clearly affects their perception of a social need for progress or development.

This section considers two major themes: the influence of the institutionalization of expectations in social relations on uncertainty attitudes, and the closely interrelated problems of cultural attitudes toward change and of entrepreneurial and managerial personality.

Institutionalization of Expectations in Social Relations

In nearly every society established values and procedures play an important part in narrowing the range of unpredictabilities. The patterns of institutionalization of expectations have varying effects on the nature, focus, and intensity of uncertainty perceptions in socio-economic situations.

The variety of these patterns may be illustrated by three simplified types of situations: paternalistic forms of authority, traditions of compromise, and institutionalized processes of conflict.

Where the authority of specific groups or persons is taken for granted and there is little social mobility, there will be less uncertainty for everybody concerning his present role and future status. Built-in paternal authority which everyone assumes to be self-evident encourages a high level of certainty in the long run. On the other hand, assertive paternalism which defensively attempts to ward off a perceived challenge to authority reflects a high level of uncertainty concerning status in the future.

Under built-in paternalism in business, expectations concerning the reactions of others to the manager's orders are rather well-defined. On the other hand, expectations concerning behavior based on compromise or institutionalized conflict involve less initial certainty. It is however true that the expectation of attitudes of compromise often has in itself a cushioning effect on uncertainty perceptions. This underlying element of stability is less likely to be present in a situation of institutionalized conflict, which tends to develop *either* toward compromise *or* toward the dominance of one group with an ensuing authoritarian situation. This is illustrated by the history of employer-labor relations in many Western societies.

In these societies, the frequency with which managers distinctly perceive cultural differences in the patterns of interaction appears to be gradually increasing. This fact points to the importance of such differences in guiding business behavior, and in limiting and selecting the areas of greatest uncertainty. Comments along these lines were indeed frequent in my interviews with managers in Western Europe, in the mid-fifties. [2]

In Great Britain, managers both of private and nationalized enterprises emphasized the deeply ingrained tradition of compromise that affects all economic relations in that country. One of them said, "We all are prepared to listen. The most difficult person in negotiation is the person who has made up his mind." Another one pointed to the "adaptability and resilience and tolerance of people" in Britain as compared with those in France, for example. A divisional manager of one of the largest corporations felt sure that its successful joint-consultation system, for instance, would not work in its French factory because managers as well as other people there are used to "fixing" things, do not believe in rules or laws, and are subject to family pressures. The chairman of another large enterprise with experience in France similarly asserted that no rules are possible there and that the entire way in which one gets cooperation is different; but he added that things differ even between regions of the British Isles. An executive of the nationalized coal industry, who had had postwar experience in German mining, pointed to the differences in reactions to discipline between the two miners' populations, including management: "In Germany everyone expects to be 'told,' otherwise they think you are soft; they don't understand innuendos, and 'orders' mean quite different things in the two countries." Some of these statements may express stereotypes, but the fact that managers in a given country perceive its cultural atmosphere as distinctive is highly important.

In Norway, there seemed to be widespread belief in a happy, satisfied way of life as a cultural goal. One of the executives thought that people were happier in Norway than in America and had more time for themselves and for social life. Another, connected with Moral Rearmament, felt that smooth cooperation among people with resulting happiness for all, was the answer to every social issue, and that this feeling was stronger in Norway than anywhere else.

In Sweden, a leader of the cooperative movement pointed to the traditions of both cooperation and disciplined organization as a distinctive trait of economic life in that country. In Germany, on the other hand, several of the executives interviewed emphasized the existing deficiencies in spontaneity and voluntary cooperation, and the need for all economic relations to be regulated by law.

In short, many managers in each country appear to be aware of specific trends in the environment in which they do business, though their perception of such trends may be less realistic in some cases than in others. The more clearcut a cultural consciousness or stereotype, the greater the uncertainties that will be evoked by any confrontation with other cultural patterns, whether in a particular business or on a larger scale.

Cultural Attitudes toward Change, and the Business Personality

Many kinds of change, either actual or anticipated, may encourage attitudes of uncertainty. Within a given culture, there may be much or little shifting of individual and group positions. At the same time, objective fluctuations of varying degree, frequency, and persistence may affect sizable parts of the population (e.g., famines and years of abundance in pre-industrial economies, or booms and depressions in modern Western societies).

Some degree of interaction exists between the cultural attitude toward such changes and their objective nature and extent. On the one hand, changes to which men are accustomed often come to be accepted insofar as they involve recognized uncertainties and ways of adjusting to them. On the other hand, a higher value placed on progress for both the individual and society (in Shackle's terminology, a high level of "imagined success"[3]) induces new requirements for the process of change.

Related differences exist between cultures that perceive legitimate alternatives to themselves and those that do not. The former may be intellectually superior and have a wider "life space," but the price they pay for it is to be far more uncertain about themselves and about the world in general.

Basic optimism is deeply ingrained in the American culture; it is practically unpatriotic to be overtly pessimistic under any circumstances. On the level of business activity, this means two things: the perception of uncertainty is likely to be less intensive than elsewhere, and to the extent that uncertainty *is* perceived, it appears as less of a threat and more of an exciting stimulus than it does in many other parts of the world.

By contrast, the typical security-consciousness of the European businessman results both in a broader and more intensive perception of uncertainty, and in a sometimes frantic effort to avoid it or to resolve it promptly and definitively. In all probability the objective job security of the European manager is greater, but so is his uncertainty perception, compared with that of his American colleague. In the past this state of mind has often expressed itself in resistance to productivity increases.[4] The chairman of a successful enterprise in Great Britain told me of his rather desperate fight against three kinds of nationwide enemies: resistance to change — the attitude that "things have always been done this way"; complacency due to prolonged prosperity — "they make good profits anyway, don't care to know whether they are the maximal ones or not"; and American aid, then still in effect, which he begged the U.S. to discontinue.

The problem of intercultural influences and possible imitation of cultural attitudes toward change and uncertainty is a crucial one. Lasting cultural change without outside influence is usually a very slow process. Within each culture, however, there may be an historical sequence of social orders and institutions which affects the quality and intensity of prevailing uncertainties in economic life. Here again there is wide variation both in the rates of autonomous change and in the attitudes toward it. Some cultures develop more successfully than others concrete mechanisms of their

74

own to handle basic changes and to readjust earlier values, if and when necessary. Kardiner contrasts for example, the increase of anxiety and hostility among the Tanala after transition from dry to wet rice cultivation (with resulting burdens on personality requirements), with the relatively smooth adjustment of the Comanche culture to an entirely new economic location, followed by actual diminution of anxieties.[5]

The injection of new elements from other cultural backgrounds usually speeds up processes of cultural change, but it also induces uncertainty with respect to social goals and roles. Such intercultural influences and comparisons can be of great importance in understanding the prevailing types of attitudes and uncertainties of business leaders.

I found much concern about this problem among German managers I interviewed. One, in charge of the personnel department of a very large enterprise, felt that the prevailing attitude in his country valued excessively academic degrees more than sound personality formation and leadership ability. But only a few miles away, the top executive of another large company declared that American methods of informal discussion and cooperation were inapplicable in Germany; that Germans function reliably only when they hear a command; and he admitted frankly that he himself liked to be the boss, to carry all the responsibility, and would not tolerate any talking back. Perhaps contemporary Germany is an outstanding example of uncertainty about basic values as they concern managerial personality requirements, largely as a result of increasing comparisons with countries whose cultural and socio-historical background is different.

One of the most important socio-historical factors in business attitudes outside North America has been the feudal legacy. Although feudalism as such has been on its way out in most parts of the world, the mentality it produced lingers on and considerably influences business, management, labor, agriculture, and politics. This applies especially to status uncertainty which results from the constant tension between the equality assumptions of economic competition and political democracy, on the one hand, and the actual restrictions and barriers to social equality, on the other. It is closely associated with the paternalistic and "familistic" traits that still characterize an important sector of enterprise in Europe, and even more so in Latin America and other modernizing areas.

Theoretically, the businessman, the farmer, the worker, the voter in Western societies are all assured of some kind of status by

75

law; practically, any of them may feel a need to assert it against a constant challenge. Such factors are not entirely absent in North America, but they are incomparably weaker there than in many other parts of the world. The feudal legacy encourages a protective mentality, with intensive uncertainty developing whenever restrictive protection threatens to weaken. Thus, the restrictive legacy of the guilds often survives in the midst of modern industrial technology. So does that part of early capitalist attitudes which interpreted ownership, among other things, as a claim to exclusive information. Educational barriers and inequalities still foster great differences in the information, as well as the capital, available to businessmen. The early capitalist wanted certainty for himself, but uncertainty for everyone else, and this attitude has not yet entirely disappeared.[6]

Business and management, like most other groups, have thus been struggling in large parts of the world with what Fromm calls "the ambiguity of freedom."[7] They have been reluctant to accept a pronounced social propensity for uncertainty as the price of freedom — at least, any uncertainty for themselves.

Uncertainty about the Economic Order and Social Leadership

Even while the feudal and "familistic" legacy was at the peak of its effectiveness, businessmen enjoyed social ascendancy. This status is now being seriously challenged in many countries, including the modernizing ones. There is no longer the assurance among businessmen that characterized them, especially in Great Britain, during the nineteenth century. Doubts have arisen concerning their function and purpose in life, the superiority of "their" society over all others, the definitive character of the progress achieved or still ahead. No longer can businessmen be sure of the prevalence of rational processes in the relations among people in general; the dominant role of the profit motive and the whole rationale of business activity; the self-adjusting character and social effects of a laissez-faire economy; and pre-established harmony in uncontrolled competitive business.

Perhaps most important of all, some doubts have arisen in the minds of businessmen, especially outside North America, concerning their natural calling to social leadership; there is greater awareness of the necessity to keep earning the claim to any such leadership through public responsibility. There has been a marked decline over the last century, again mainly outside North America, of certainty regarding the permanence of a capitalistic order regardless of its performance. As mentioned earlier, this order (however defined) is under heavy attack in the modernizing areas, not to mention the communist countries.

The defensiveness of upper classes even in the face of objective success is a phenomenon of great importance in our period. Two hundred years ago the *ancien régime* perceived itself, including its social stratification, as the only natural and possible order, which nobody would think of challenging. Even the British capitalism of a hundred years ago had a somewhat similar attitude, or at least it did not care very much whether someone ventured to challenge it:

Today things are different. In the United States the upper groups, which are largely identical with business, are now rather defensive, although this attitude is perhaps less intensive and certainly more hidden from themselves and from others than it is in other parts of the world. In Europe, business has been stricken for a long time by a severe malaise. The situation is similar in Asia and Latin America. This malaise is far older than the rise of communism, although the latter has clearly contributed to it.

Schumpeter thought that both this malaise and the underlying external challenge were a result of intrinsic traits of capitalism. [8] At any rate, even in periods of its greatest economic success capitalistic business does not seem able to free itself of an underlying uncertainty, if not pessimism, about its own future.

Part of this uncertainty may express a collective guilt feeling that goes back to the very origins of the order, to the disintegration of medieval values that were not replaced by an equally well-defined system of new values. To the uncertainty in early and later capitalism on how to reconcile the requirements of business action with various religious and ethical codes, there has been added more recent uncertainty among businessmen concerning their own motives and basic purposes. Profit (or money) is not as often seen as the ultimate driving force in life that it used to be. This uncertainty has now been compounded by the widespread rejection by the young of business values and old rationality concepts, and by the cleavage between their lagging motivation to study and social needs for trained manpower.

The role of long-range expectations has been changing to some extent. Survival and growth of the enterprise, with assured employment for its trained personnel, are now frequently stressed over short-run profits. At the same time, awareness of social responsibility, with some uncertainty about its concrete range, has been growing.[9] The prevailing codes of business conduct have been changing, even in we allow for frequent rationalizations and advertising stunts. In my interviews with managers in Western Europe, I found nearly everywhere an emphasis on the community consciousness of management. This aim was accepted by representatives of private, cooperative, and nationalized enterprises alike; and the real argument seemed to concern the type of enterprise and the specific ways in which this accepted aim could best be fulfilled. This is far from the old charisma of the upper class based on unchallengeable privileges. Even so, considerable vacillation in the judgment of business about its own rights and duties remains everywhere.

The urge of management for social approval has been increasing in the course of history but has been met only in an uncertain, fluctuating, and possibly diminishing way. In industrialized countries, at least, managers are anxious to prove to the public and to themselves not only that their methods are efficient, but that their enterprise is socially useful. In some industries, such claims take quite an amount of rationalization, yet they are seldom absent. The attitude of accountability and the urge to perform continuously are far from the older unconditional certainty of status. There is also a constant attempt to overcome the suspicions of intellectuals about business. More generally, there is widespread fear of hostility toward business (or the capitalist order) that might be caused by *either* success or failure. This fear of hostility is extensive even in the United States. Yet an objective survey of criticisms there in the early fifties showed that the great majority of people clearly emphasized the beneficial effects of businessmen's activities over the adverse effects.[10]

The greatest concrete challenge to management, business, or the capitalist order has come from the labor movement. Here again, management's perception of this challenge has not necessarily been in line with reality. Nor does "labor movement" mean the same thing in every part of the world. The traditional focus of American trade unionism on immediate improvements *within* the prevailing economic order has been in direct contrast to the political and ideological aims of labor organizations in Europe, Asia, or Latin America, especially those of a Marxian, Fabian, or religious type. In all cases, however, labor movements have contributed much to management's feeling of general uncertainty simply by presenting an explicit or implicit challenge to formerly uncontested claims of business to social leadership, prestige, and status.

There have been unmistakable effects on management resulting in feelings of fear, envy, doubt about the future, even "status panic," to use Mills' term.[11] The uncertainty far exceeds doubts about the future amount of labor costs, or about an uninterrupted work process in the plant. It is the control of management over the enterprise, and the social status of the management group as a whole that are perceived as being at stake. This fact explains some of the defensive responses of management toward labor unions and parties, and the frequent fear of communism even when there is no factual basis for it.

Finally, with increased size and complexity of the enterprise, and trained hired management gradually replacing individual entrepreneurship, some kinds of uncertainties affecting business leadership have become more intricate. This applies to professional managers in public enterprise as well as private. The situation has been described by one professional manager as follows: "Managerial enterprise is at once complex and more difficult to operate than either free enterprise or monopoly. Its functioning impinges on all its members adding a new series of strains. The tensions and anxieties of management are wearing...These strains are not compensated by immediate tangible accomplishment. The joy of attaining a definite goal has been submerged in the vastness of space and time. Management must learn to get its satisfaction vicariously, trusting that its contribution will sometime fructify to the benefit of the community as well as to the enterprise."[12]

In other words, uncertainties underlying managerial action are less frequently resolved by its results becoming visible; results may not become visible for a long time. Meanwhile, additional uncertainties may appear *within* the management structure. The earlier kind of ambiguity in every market situation may sometimes be reduced today, only to be replaced by the new ambiguity of one's position and prospects within the large firm. This may be intensified by the rootlessness of numerous executives who keep moving from one job and community to another in their search for continuous promotion.

Political Processes and Business Uncertainty

In countries where the future of the socio-economic order and of the social role of management is not subject to explicit doubts, there may still be a considerable impact of political processes upon business uncertainty. To begin with, politics is often perceived in terms of the vagaries of an incessant struggle for personal and group power, not in terms of a public debate on the best way to assure the common good. Political parties — especially those that are not based on a permanent ideology and organization — are often seen as constantly shifting with regard to economic policies.

Most of all, "the government" is frequently perceived by businessmen as a reckless monster that is their natural enemy, not as the chosen executive agency of a democratic society. Government regulation and the threat of future interventions challenge the businessman's time-honored system of beliefs, arouse frustrations due to the limitation of his accustomed choices, and foster a feeling of role deprivation and lowered status in the community. Intervention leads to fundamental uncertainty about the future of the economic order even when there is no thought of nationalization. Wherever nationalization does occur, it often changes little in the activities of the managers directly concerned, but appears to many others as a glaring symbol of challenge to their accustomed role in society.

Regulation alone may contain an element of greater certainty from the viewpoint of the businessman, to the extent that it is felt to reduce uncertainties from other sources, such as lack of adequate information or absence of accepted standards of conduct. [13] Such regulation may also resolve uncertainties resulting from the political and legislative process, although it often takes additional decisions on the administrative and judicial levels to achieve this effect. Even so, the top executive, in the judgment of one of them, "is increasingly surrounded by legalistic, economic, and technological problems which he cannot possibly comprehend except with the aid of experts (and perhaps not then) but with which he must deal in the over-all decisions of business... He does what he is paid for: makes his own guess based on his own experience and judgment and awaits the consequences." [14]

What can we say about the kind of government that is run by businessmen, not just through informal influences but through direct administrative responsibility? Insofar as the evidence goes — mainly in the United States — it is not very encouraging. The initial reaction of many managers to the Eisenhower administration was a feeling of relief; but it turned out to be difficult to keep men with business background in the government over prolonged periods, and more difficult to get them adjusted to the requirements of public administration.

The fluctuations of taxation are especially important because of their economic and emotional effect on business uncertainty. There is considerable evidence that executives are actually affected to a very limited extent by taxes in their daily effort and performance, [15] but the intrusion into the privacy of business conduct and the implied challenge from external supervision to the social leadership of business are deeply resented — in contrast to voluntary self-taxation for philanthropic or political purposes. Moreover, taxation is traditionally exposed to severe struggles and fluctuations in the course of the parliamentary process.

At the other end of the scale, there is a long history of government subsidies, direct or indirect, to private business in very many countries; but here again such benefits have often been affected by political uncertainties and fluctuations. Tariffs have usually been designed to give domestic producers the assurance of lessened competition and more profitable operation, but they have been exposed to the vagaries of political conflicts and, sometimes, to foreign retaliation.

A good many businessmen and managers now consider a "Keynesian" policy of monetary correctives to the process of competition more reassuring and stable than the old system, but others are profoundly disquieted by the implied challenge to the perfect nature and, thereby, certainty of the automatism as originally assumed. Another area of legislative, administrative, and judicial action that evokes uncertainty in some countries is antitrust policy. This involves both the basic assumptions and goals of this policy, and future interpretations of antitrust provisions as they relate to various business practices.

Business reactions to the expanding welfare activities of modern governments have also been ambivalent. On the one hand, social security, public housing, conservation, farm supports, labor legislation, and public power policy are widely seen as putting a floor under the well-being of the nation; on the other hand, such measures have often been perceived as a threat to business because of their tendency to call for ever more intervention without any definite end in sight. In the United States, the Tennessee Valley Authority, which in its own area has been widely interpreted by business as an assurance of growing prosperity, has been seen by many Northern and Midwestern businessmen as a factor of uncertainty concerning the whole future of private enterprise, simply by setting an alternative or precedent. Attitudes encountered in Western European countries were rather different, especially in Sweden where the prevailing view was expressed by the chief manager of a very large company as follows: "We are for private enterprise and initiative and all that, but we have always believed that where the risk of private firms taking undue advantage of their position exists, and where the national interest is concerned, the state should exercise control. We look at the state not as a hydra but as 'ourselves'." Such identification is likely to greatly reduce the perception of present or future state action as a factor of uncertainty.

Perhaps such perception would be less frequent or intensive if it were not for the experiences with totalitarianism discussed in Chapter 2 that various parts of the world have had during the last few decades. The expansion of political action into an all-embracing state, either in fascist or communist form, has posed for many a crucial question concerning the limits of public intervention. Such fears are often unjustified where traditions of democracy are strong, but this does not make them ineffective. Totalitarianism has brought a new dimension of uncertainty, even to populations that have not experienced it directly. It has shown how vulnerable and perishable the most basic values of a nation can be unless it knows how to preserve them actively and relentlessly.

Managerial responses to the whole phenomenon of totalitarianism have varied widely according to person and country. Some people have not been affected by it at all or have confined themselves to reactions outside their business activities. Others have been gripped by a pervasive fear of whatever they perceive as communism, and in some cases have endorsed "loyalty" and "security" programs which have led to extreme uncertainty for nearly everybody in the plant and have eventually backfired on management itself. Generally, pressures for conformity within management have been extensive, and in a nation with traditions of freedom such pressures mean uncertainty and often insecurity for everybody. In still other, more extreme cases, this state of mind has led to support of fascist demagogues or groups expected to resolve all uncertainties.[16] In Nazi Germany, the expectation of "being told" at all times provided a degree of certainty in specific situations, but only at the price of generalizing other uncertainties — those concerning the next phase of the Führer's intuition. When it was found through sad experience that even a totalitarian regime could not "help" by providing constant certainty, a frequent result was apathy or cynicism.

In summary, the combined world impact of communism and fascism on the Western world has resulted in an intensified atmosphere of long-range uncertainty in which managerial reactions and decisions must take place.

War, Technology, and Uncertainty

To the impact of totalitarian experiences must be added the effects of two world wars in a generation and of renewed threats of war at a time of a rapidly changing science and technology. In the United States, the productive capacity of both industry and agriculture had expanded rapidly under the pressure of war. Industrial growth has continued since World War II along with prevailing prosperity; but most farmers, after years of high incomes and successful mechanization, still cling to government supports. The wartime expansion of money circulation and federal debt has meanwhile become a permanent feature of the U.S. economy, but continues to cause great concern to many businessmen who have difficulty in distinguishing between private principles, such as thrift and solvency at all times, and the requirements of public monetary policy.

The aftermath of World War II has also been characterized by unprecedented forms and amounts of foreign aid. All this has meant for American business not only a flow of orders on foreign aid accounts, but also new and untested business situations, especially in modernizing areas. The role of world power that had been thrown into America's lap, and the uncertainty concerning the best way to carry out this tempting but potentially dangerous function, also affected the atmosphere of business activities.

In the 1950s and 1960s the threat of yet another world war led to more widespread uncertainty about the future. Even those who did not interpret the Korean conflict as the beginning of a world war could never be certain after the summer of 1950 just how long the peace or, at least, the cold phase of war could be maintained. These doubts have been multiplied by the Vietnam war and the chronic Mideastern crisis.

The possibility of a major war is brought home to business in the U.S. and elsewhere by the permanent war economy in peacetime, which has come to characterize our period. Drastic restrictions, it is true, are on the whole confined to times of acute military conflict. But the enormous U.S. federal budget, of which over 80% expresses either directly or indirectly the continuing costs of World War II and the expenditures for current military requirements, the corresponding tax load, government purchases and subsidies based on military considerations, strategic controls of foreign trade, and countless other measures, constantly remind management of the uncertain character of peace. In addition, the threat of possible controls of a more restrictive nature, of drastic wartime taxes, and of the inflationary effects of armaments always remains.

Under these conditions, accustomed patterns of business conduct and expectations in an industrialized economy are ever less in line with the realities of the period. Consumer preferences, market competition, risk calculations based on past experiences, all become highly uncertain guides for managerial decisions in those fields of business that are directly affected by military requirements at any given time. In a period that is neither peace nor war, two conflicting principles of economic activity actually compete with one another — for example, in decisions on whether to trade with a particular country. Whenever the decision is left to the management of an individual company, it may find itself in a quandary.

In addition, one must consider the effects of recent or imminent advances in science and technology on economic life. Atomic energy is about to upset many previous calculations of energy costs. Work with radioactive materials presents to industry unprecedented problems of protection and waste disposal, and the hydrogen bomb carried by long-range missiles threatens total destruction in case of another major war. In the field of aviation, jet and rocket technology, supersonic aircraft, and space travel may be the most dramatic developments of today and tomorrow, but the effect of the helicopter upon the economy may well turn out to be far more sweeping. Scientific farming may be supported, in the near future, by partial control of the weather. Automation has been changing the basis of employment policy and labor relations, and is now profoundly affecting office work, including managerial activities. Huge electronic computers are supposed to take chance out of many executive decisions, but the problem of feeding them with the right kind of data may survive.

Chemistry is breaking into ever more of the established industries, ranging from textiles to building materials, and encroachment has become frequent among other industries as well. Nearly every giant corporation and many smaller ones have been expanding into unexpected fields. Biology has just begun to make its full imprint on nutrition, health, and the related areas of mass con-

84

sumption. Air conditioning has changed the work and living habits of people, and affects the location of industries. Mass media and the uses of applied psychology in the office, including the managerial office, may be further expanded, for good or bad.

Scientific and technological progress is nothing new, of course, but we have apparently broken through the initial barriers in some important fields and can expect far more rapid changes than have occurred in the past. Detailed information about managerial perceptions of this situation is scarce, but there are indications that it is seen in terms of a hope *and* a threat, and that it has generally increased the feeling of uncertainty concerning the future. Environmental protection, in particular, is widely feared to impose on management ill-defined technical and financial requirements.

It is the *combination* of the two kinds of developments discussed — continuing war threats along with rapid changes in science and technology — that affects most deeply the general atmosphere of business activities. In this situation, management is engaged in a widespread search for security devices, either on its own or with government aid. Some factories go below the surface of the earth, or at least are dispersed outside the urban centers of industry. Government orders are often solicited or at least eagerly accepted, not out of patriotism alone but because they come from a customer who may last longer than the peacetime consumer market.

There are, of course, past examples of company expansion stimulated by military needs, and the defense argument for tariffs and subsidies is age-old. In the history of large corporations in such fields as chemicals, steel, oil, and automotive equipment, armaments and wars have been a decisive driving force of expansion. In our own period, however, the urge for quick expansion reflects in part, at least, concern about the durability of peace, impatience with the past rate of technological innovation, worry about keeping up with the rapid rate of change, and general uncertainty about the future. Business expands partly in a desire to "beat" this uncertainty if possible.

Modernization Aspirations and Investment

The atmosphere of uncertainty is probably more contagious today among the nations of the world than it has ever been before. This is no longer a matter of the continuing economic impact of World War II, or the general frustrations experienced by victors as

85

well as vanquished. There are various uncertainties that affect international business relations more specifically.

For one thing, the virtual end of colonialism has brought considerable losses for Western investors and a high degree of uncertainty for remaining foreign investments. Some of the new regimes in Latin America, Asia, and Africa are characterized by great political instability along with intensive nationalism, based in part on the past evils of foreign economic domination. The capital needs of these countries are urgent, but the uncertainties facing foreign investors are forbidding.

Second, though inflation and monetary instability in the world have on the whole been manageable in recent years, they remain a substantial factor in business uncertainty and a potential threat for the future. As long as it remains uncertain whether and when a given currency will be freely convertible, and on what terms, international trade and investment remain subject to unforseeable influences.

Third, there is increased realization of the complex problems facing international investment for reasons of political, social, and cultural variations of a lasting type. Business principles that are perceived in one part of the world as vigorous initiative and sound competition have been interpreted elsewhere as political interference, greedy exploitation, or destruction of time-honored ways of life. Such experiences have made the prospective foreign investor a far more wary man than was his predecessor some decades ago. At the same time, new inter-governmental agencies, such as the World Bank Group, have been moving into some of those areas of investment that involve dealings with inscrutable political agencies abroad or that present other excessive uncertainties from the viewpoint of private export capital.

Fourth, the aspirations of the poorer nations have brought a new and still largely untested element into the world investment situation. The urge for modernization is far more widespread and intensive now than it has been in the past. So has been, until recently, the expectation of aid from the industrialized nations, especially from the United States or Soviet Russia. Private management is facing a challenge here for which there are few precedents in its experience. To what extent is it *its* business to aid the poorer countries in their endeavor to modernize, and under what conditions is there profit in it? How exactly should one go about it, and what should be the sequence of measures involving transportation, housing, nutrition, health, education, power supply, light industries, heavy industries, and distribution? To what extent do foreign investors need to take into account the cultural values and differences among the populations concerned, and how well equipped are they to do so? All these questions involve a strong element of uncertainty.

The wealthier nations now see the wide gap between population growth and essential production in much of Asia, Africa, Latin America, and Southern Europe as a challenge and potential threat to themselves, and here again private management is just beginning to consider whether and in what ways this situation should be of specific concern to it. At the same time, the rapidly changing uses and meanings of "raw materials," in the light of the sudden importance of uranium, for instance, have increased the potential interest of Western business in what was formerly considered a hopelessly backward type of area. With a greater awareness of the responsibilities of industrialized nations, a frequent feeling of uneasiness and instability tends to affect the atmosphere of business activities in these countries.

Uncertainty and Economic Fluctuations

There are, in addition, continuing internal influences in the industrialized countries that encourage a feeling of perennial short-run instability or suspense despite prolonged business prosperity. The largely favorable experience of recent years has not been sufficient to wipe out entirely the recollection of the disastrous depression of the 1930s or, for that matter, the inflationary trends of the following decades. The belief in an everlasting prosperity, which was so widespread 50 years ago, apparently has not been restored in full. It may be more frequent among the younger businessmen, who have known only postwar prosperity, than among older ones, who think more about the vagaries of business fluctuations and perhaps also about the financial problems for individuals arising from the lengthening span of life.

Continuous uncertainty concerning the durability of prosperity differs from the intrinsic uncertainty that is implicit in the competitive process and, indeed, is largely created by it. This latter type of uncertainty is usually associated by business with a dynamic economy, as well as with the continuous fight of each firm for survival against under-selling, innovations, or restrictive practices of others. Uncertainty concerning business fluctuations, on the other hand, is expressed in wariness with respect to possible deflation or inflation that might affect everybody , or other factors of instability. Both kinds of uncertainty help explain the continuing trend to merger and conglomeration of enterprises, which in turn increases the uncertainty for others.

An investigation made by the Survey Research Center in the United States led to the following conclusion: "It is important to note that people who express uncertainty regarding the business outlook are *not* simply a group of sensible people who refuse to make a guess about the future. This group (those expressing uncertainty) has attitudes toward buying conditions similar to those held by the group which is pessimistic about the long-range business outlook. In other words, these people are not confident that prosperity will last; therefore, they desire to save and question the wisdom of making major postponable expenditures." [17]

Similar considerations may affect business investment policy. Among tentative conclusions from empirical research are the following:

"Uncertainty about the future of a pessimistic economic outlook may...impede investment, not only by causing businessmen to turn down opportunities after consideration, but also by making them unable to perceive opportunities." [18]

"When a baffling change puts in an appearance, there seems to be a natural tendency among some business executives to start whistling in the dark." [19] On the other hand, there is some evidence of an increasing tendency on the part of large (especially multinational) corporations to "look across" fluctuations in the national economy and adopt a long-run viewpoint in investment policy. The long view does not seem sufficiently prevalent, however, to check the interaction of strong uncertainty perceptions with the business situation, especially through the medium of cumulative investment decisions.

Sombart and Knight long ago pointed to the historical fight for greater certainty of business action through the growth of general insurance-mindedness. [20] Others see a trend toward increasing business certainty through improved forecasting; a well defined probability is expected to encourage action even when a forecast is adverse. On the other hand, uncertainty, including the kind that is rooted in either cyclical or secular instabilities, is seen by some as an indispensable stimulus for business initiative and progress.

To the extent that the "depression psychosis," to use Galbraith's term, [21] has survived years of prevailing prosperity, it

88

interacts with underlying doubts about the future of the economic order, the social function of private management, and the state of the world. Progress in the technological and financial sense thus has not done away with the general atmosphere of uncertainty, and in some respects has added to it.

Summary and Conclusions

This discussion should not be construed as implying that there is nothing but uncertainty in the present world, or that business action in industrialized as well as in newly modernizing countries is influenced exclusively by an atmosphere of uncertainty. In some respects Western business today can base its decisions on greater certainty that it could in the past, for example, in determining expansion or plant location through more advanced techniques of calculation and planning. To this extent a manager may feel more nearly "certain" that he is doing the right thing (if not the optimal thing) than his predecessors could. He is exposed, however, to powerful influences from culture and society far beyond his firm's control or insight. These influences act upon his own attitudes, role expectations, and general values, as well as upon those of his colleagues and competitors. The specific ways in which a social atmosphere of uncertainty actually influences the everyday conduct of business require much further exploration.

With this aim in mind, the preceding discussion can be summarized as follows:

The perception of uncertainties is greatly influenced by the cultural setting and the corresponding scale of values, including the impact of culture on the distribution of specific types of personality. In the American culture, basic optimism greatly influences the setting of business activities. It is in contrast with the security-mindedness of other populations and their businessmen. A feudal legacy, in particular, often fosters status uncertainties and antagonisms, such as those expressed in a late stage of defensive paternalism.

In recent decades, the business atmosphere has been subject to rapid changes nearly everywhere. The social leadership of business has been challenged, and the nature of management itself has changed. In many countries, the old assurance of the upper classes has given way to a malaise. They have become rather defensive and, at the same time , increasingly uncertain about their basic values, a situation which has sometimes resulted in an increased urge for social approval.

Political processes have greatly influenced business uncertainty, especially in countries where business has traditionally perceived government as a threat. Public regulation may increase objective certainty factors, but it may also be seen by business as a challenge to its social role and leadership. This applies especially to financial policies, including taxation, subsidies, monetary measures, and also to antitrust, environment and welfare policies when they are viewed as determined by the vagaries of politics.

In recent decades, international experiences with totalitarianism have brought a new dimension of uncertainty to the business world. So have two world wars in a generation along with renewed uncertainty about the future of the peace, the rapid pace of technological advance, the fact that the world economy has generally been in a state of uneasy transition toward unknown goals, and the prevalence of conflicting ideologies and political unrest in many parts of the world, prominently including the modernizing areas.

Finally, fear of economic fluctuations continues to be important in the industrialized countries because of persistent memories of the 1930s and added fears of inflation.

In conclusion, influences that foster uncertainty feelings in the general population, along with additional influences that mainly affect business management, are widespread in contemporary society. Future research needs to explore more fully the specific ways in which business attitudes and managerial actions in various parts of the world are influenced by this social atmosphere. But there is little doubt that business and management in modernizing areas are subject to such influences no less than are their colleagues in the West, though the specific patterns may be different. Special attitudinal aspects of business management in modernizing areas will be discussed in the next chapter.

CHAPTER 5

Managerial Attitudes and the Quest for Modernization

From the discussion, in the preceding chapter, of socio-psychological factors in business uncertainty under the conditions of industrialized economies, we now turn to managerial attitudes in newly modernizing areas and the impact of these attitudes on the modernization process. Consequently, this chapter is focussed on the formation of managerial and business groups in modernizing countries, their attitudinal structure, the ways in which their mode of thinking can influence developmental processes, and the possibilities for public policy to incorporate managerial attitudes into a national or regional program for modernization.

It has sometimes been assumed that enterprise managers, given certain kinds of training, skills, or education in general, will behave in the same way no matter *where* these qualities are to be applied. Interestingly, this appears to be the semi-conscious assumption of some managerial organizations in less developed countries. No such assumption is made here. We shall merely discuss the extent to which managerial skills or attitudes from industrialized economies actually lend themselves to application in modernizing areas. The attitudes of managers toward their own function and toward society in general *may* differ according to the cultural setting, social structure, phase of modernization, and personality of the individual concerned. We shall not assume, therefore, that managers anywhere represent the closest available approximation to economic man.

This leaves the question of whether or not modernization policy *needs* to consider cultural, social, or historical variables in the attitudes of managers in various countries. Are the newly modernizing countries today passing through phases of management or entrepreneurship that parallel the economic history of the now industrialized nations, or do those countries experience largely different trends due to elapsed time, the "demonstration effect," cultural differences, or any other factors?

The following considerations are based in the main on Latin American materials, including a detailed study of managerial attitudes in Chile and numerous interviews with managers, businessmen, and economists in other countries, but there are broader applications.[1]

Management, "Entrepreneurial Spirit," and Family

Managerial attitudes represent both a wider and a narrower concept than an entrepreneurial spirit does. We are here concerned both with the managers who show such spirit and those who do not. The presence of entrepreneurial initiative within a framework of managerial attitudes does represent, of course, a highly significant facet of these attitudes. [2]

It is important, however, to beware of ethnocentric interpretations. The prevailing value system in a community may either encourage or discourage innovation and individual initiative; it may confine such opportunities to a socio-economic and cultural élite. This is exemplified by the extreme difficulty an Indian of the South American *altiplano* faces in ever becoming an entrepreneur even within his own community, let alone the Peruvian or Equadorian economy as a whole.

Another reservation is in order concerning the relationship between entrepreneurship and private ownership. In many modernizing countries in our period, the major initiative for economic innovation comes from a government agency; planning officials and politicians assume here most of the real risk that is involved in such initiative.

The challenge facing public policy in these countries consists partly of providing sufficient training facilities and of breaking down rigid social barriers which may impede the recruitment of new managers. Public policy can also encourage — through tax benefits, awards, or decorations — innovative behavior and a willingness to assume responsibility and risk in economic matters. But each government will be acting in an area which is limited by the cultural and socio-historical background of its country.

In Western Europe and North America, much family influence in business has survived, but there has been a strong trend toward trained professional management. In less developed countries, the initial social status of managerial activities may be low. Managerial skills are rare and the role of foreigners and recent immigrants in management is considerable. This role sometimes makes managers stand out as a somewhat alien element within the national economy. Among the managers of native background, a strong feudal or pre-industrial legacy is often noticeable. They are quite likely to come from the families of large landowners and to retain some landowning interests themselves along with being active in industry or commerce. This activity may result in the preponderance of the family in a given field of business, but this does not necessarily mean specialization. A man or family who has money available will look for *some* opportunity to invest it promptly and profitably, and the specific decision is more likely to depend on personal contacts than on expert knowledge of a specific field of enterprise.

Some combination of paternalism and authoritarianism in the practice of management is very frequent in the less developed countries, although the degree varies considerably. The professionalization of management, which has made rapid headway in North America and Western Europe, has only recently begun even in countries like Argentina and is nonexistent at this point in many others. A strict division between the board of directors and the executive staff is rare. It is usually taken for granted that the manager should hold stock in the company. In those cases in which the real power of decision is held by the board of directors, the firm is likely to be a family enterprise.

Whatever the balance of its advantages and drawbacks may be, the family enterprise is still strongly entrenched, although the historical trend appears to lead gradually away from it. It often adapts itself to changing times by switching to competent, professionally trained managers but also tries to train some younger members of the family for the same role or to have promising trained managers marry into the family. Success of the firm becomes a device to enhance the social status of the family, its differentiation from lower groups of society and "competing" rival families, and its political influence. Conversely, family status and political influence often enhance success in business.

The inter-connection between family status, business management, and politics continues to characterize most of the less developed nations. Sooner or later, this situation turns out to be a limiting factor in modernization. It limits the overall supply and specific selection of competent managerial personnel, and may also reduce the clarity and flexibility of management. These attributes characterize the owner-manager system (especially in partnership) more often when it does *not* rely on family links. Family management tends to blur the division of labor among executives even when the size of the enterprise would permit and require such division. This may lead to lack of defined functions and to arbitrariness in any delegation of authority. Finally, family considerations may assume an economically unjustified role in the location of the firm and other important business decisions.

Location, Prestige, and Markets

In modernizing countries, decisions on the location of firms have not often been guided by the yardsticks that are traditionally indicated in economic textbooks from the West, such as the proximity of raw materials or consumer markets, or the availability of transportation facilities and plentiful labor.

Initially, it is true, native-owned industries in modernizing countries are quite often adjuncts of farm production: Canneries, sugar refineries, coffee-roasting plants, meat-freezing facilities, wool or cotton mills. Wealthy landowning families convince themselves that such industrial facilities would add to their income and prestige. This agrarian basis of industries, often connected with ownership of wholesale commerce and transportation services, leads to a strong tendency to concentrate business activites in the area where the family resides and enjoys prestige. Expansion into other areas may follow, but abstract concepts of purely economic criteria in the location of business firms remain rather alien to the basic mentality of the emerging managerial groups in modernizing countries.

In addition, the family character of the initial landownership impedes the formation of a professional group of agricultural managers. The owner *may* acquire expert knowledge in this activity, but this is not always the case. Only recently, with the growth of absentee ownership and more diversified business interests of some landowners, has there been a somewhat clearer tendency toward the employment of professional farm managers, in such countries as Argentina.

94

Diversification has usually been encouraged by the persistent expectation of a *small* market for any given product or enterprise. This is especially true of the countries with a "dual economy," such as Peru and Equador. It is usually assumed by the managers of enterprises there that the Indians of the *altiplano* and the Amazon, who constitute the majority of the population, will never understand what modern industrial products are for, and will never have the cash to buy them; the new urban proletariat of recent Indian origin (the *cholos*) is not considered very differently.

Therefore, most managers believe that high prices and profits are indispensable in dealing with that minority of the population that is able and willing to buy their goods. Aggregate demand is judged to be so inelastic, upwardly at least, that price reductions and low profit per unit would be ineffective, if not dangerous, in that they would reduce the capital accumulation of enterprises and, thus, their ability to survive and expand. Moreover, advertising might make the consumers suspicious and might generally run afoul of the unwritten codes of proper business behavior. This is also true of any ardent or "excessive" competition. A Brazilian manager I interviewed contributed a nice rationalization by suggesting high tariffs against Japanese goods "for reasons of consumer psychology," even though his company admittedly did not need such protection! Admiration for the competitive results of American or European industry is accompanied by regretful assurances that this lofty principle is unfortunately inapplicable to a poor country.

For similar reasons, high productivity is still thought of quite often as a luxury which only rich countries with a big market can afford — not as the basis of wealth. Why should a country with a small market waste money and effort on stepping up productivity if there is nobody to buy additional goods thus produced?

A good many managers, it is true, are willing to expand production if and when there has been *previous* evidence of expanding demand. But a mental association between profit and market size often does not exist, or the profit urge itself assumes forms rather different from those in America or Europe.

Profit in Modernizing Countries

Even in advanced economies, the role of the profit motive in management has often been overrated, or there has been insufficient clarity concerning the possible meanings of profit, especially the difference between short-range and long-range considerations and between *making* a profit (even a high one) and *maximizing* profit. [3]

In modernizing countries, the prevailing attitude toward profit remains governed by the desire of many to get rich quick and then to live happily — that is, idly — ever after. A Peruvian banker characterized the predominant attitude among his customers as follows: "Why should I wait for profit for three or four years when it is immediately available in a big way, and when everyone else expects immediate profit?"

At this time, the extreme short-range view still predominates, especially in smaller firms, even when expansion is thought of in a general way. A variety of reasons is given to explain the impossibility of long-range considerations even when there are investment intentions. Inflationary experiences and dangers are mentioned in various countries: in Chile, for instance, where they have been endemic since the nineteenth century. Political instability — meaning anything from chronic change of ministers and development plans to social revolution — is also cited frequently. One must make a profit promptly while one's friends are still in the government. More permanent or structural reasons are also emphasized: the national character, chronic economic stagnation, or the dependence of the country on fluctuating world markets for its chief export product, and sometimes on the vagaries of the climate and crops as well. Mentioned also are the smallness and vulnerability of the domestic market, and the need for immediate huge profits as the only possible source of investment where management operates in an inadequate and constantly changing environment.

Undoubtedly there is some truth in all the reasons given for the short-range approach, but there is also a good deal of rationalization. The reasons given are mostly valid to *some* extent but not quite as valid or permanent as they are claimed to be, and not always a convincing excuse for inefficiency or high prices. At any rate, such concepts from Europe and America as "confidence," "risk," "expectations," and "uncertainty" should only be used with extreme care in modernizing countries.

Unless such categories, derived from a Western background, are only used in a purely formal sense, they will rarely fit the attitudinal framework that characterizes managers in modernizing countries. "Expectations" are influenced here in an incomparably greater degree by nonmarket factors such as family status, political pull or instability, social unrest, or the outlook for peace or war in the world. "Uncertainty," in addition to meaning an objective impossibility of knowing or evaluating fully a competitive market situation, includes the extreme difficulty of sizing up the effect of the weather on the next harvest, the fluctuations of the world market for the single export crop, and the possibility of a *junta* or popular rebellion taking over the government by force.

Similarly, "risk" refers not only to incompletely defined hazards, but to the possibility that the total assets of a firm or an individual, even his life, may be lost suddenly — , therefore, one should try to avoid it. "Confidence," under these conditions, refers not merely to an affirmative evaluation of specific market prospects or even of the prospects of prosperity in a strictly economic sense, but to an overall picture of promising factors in the political, international, social, and economic outlook for the nation and area.

The parameters of profit expectation, therefore, differ considerably from those in more advanced economies. On the one hand, any "rational" drive for profit maximization would look like an impossible proposition, since so many influences cannot be sized up, let alone calculated, with any degree of exactness. On the other hand, the predominant aim is very high profit without much concern for its maximization. There is strong desire to achieve it quickly without much effort or thought toward the more distant future.

This attitude is enhanced by the frequent inadequacy of "external economies" in less developed countries. When public arrangements and services such as water and power supply, transportation, housing, repair and market facilities cannot be counted on in a sufficient degree, the motivation or apparent justification for quick high profit rises. Also, the objective need for resourcefulness on the part of the management to provide some of these facilities on its own is increasing, although this does not necessarily mean that management is always aware of this need and ready to meet it. Why spend money and effort on the maintenance of equipment if future conditions are uncertain and risky? The whole idea that management, either private or public, must essentially rely on its own ingenuity — rather than on being supported or subsidized from above — is still fairly rare in these countries (and some more advanced ones, too). This idea, however, has been making headway in recent years.

Cultural Variations in Managerial Attitudes

In their attitudes toward the government, short-range profit, and the uncertainties and risks facing them, the managers of each country are inevitably — although often unconsciously — influenced by the cultural setting and the prevailing system of values. [4]

In certain countries, managers are likely to view the problems of their enterprise or those of the economy as strictly national in character. For instance, the degree to which they see capital shortage or social radicalism as "Chilean" or "Peruvian," rather than as "Latin American" or "developmental" varies considerably. So does their perception — optimistic, pessimistic, or detached — of national, cultural, or regional characteristics of the population and of the outlook for modernization. Sometimes the prevailing interpretation of such characteristics emphasizes cooperative and intelligent traits of the population; in other cases it concentrates on supposedly lazy, greedy, or apathetic attitudes of the people.

In my Chilean investigation of managerial attitudes, one of the questions I asked was, "Are there specific Chilean traits which influence business?" All but two of the seventy managers who expressed a definite opinion thought that there are such traits, either favorable (such as intelligence) or unfavorable (such as negligence). Interestingly, foreign-born managers evaluated Chilean traits slightly more favorably than did those born in the country.

We are not implying, of course, that such perceptions on the part of managers are necessarily realistic or accurate. What matters is that these perceptions and the cultural mentality which they express, are bound to influence the attitudinal structure and motivation of managers in each country, thus coloring their view of the possibilities of modernization and of their own role in it.

Traditional emphasis in a country on nonmaterial values is likely to slow down, if not prevent, the rise of systematic business management in the Western sense. A strong influence of caste mentality is likely to have similar effects as does the concentration of material interests on consumption, especially luxury consumption in the upper classes, rather than production and service. Where leisure, contemplation, an unhurried way of going about things, and avoidance of worry about the future represent predominant values in life, precise split-second decisions or rigid deadlines may be at odds with cultural assumptions. In fact, they may be incompatible with the personal touch and the informal utilization of political or family contacts which are traditionally essential to the conduct of business in these countries.

98

Cultural variations also need to be taken into account by public development policy and by foreign aid, for instance, in the *timing* of "sound" measures or the degree of pressure used. Even tax incentives and subsidies may be interpreted as mere handouts unless cultural values favor the rise of systematic management or can be adjusted sufficiently to favor it. Foreign aid, similarly, may sometimes miss the point by merely sending foreign textbooks and management experts. There *is* a certain field of effectiveness for purely technical advice, but even here the possibilities are rather limited in the absence of an attitude that recognizes the importance of such values as "exactness" and "reliability." Abstract organization charts are of little effect where management is based primarily on family relations and personal contacts. But these relations and contacts can be brought into a certain order and be made subservient in some degree to the requirements of efficient management.

Personality and Managerial Effectiveness

The person who shows independent judgment and originality can expect a rapid rise in one kind of society and complete failure in another. This is especially true in newly modernizing economies where the margin between success and failure tends to be thin and where subjectivism in judging economic questions prevails.

In these countries, the division between a person's managerial and other interests and activities is often vague. A man is quite likely to devote part of his office hours to politics or family affairs. He may make important managerial decisions while visiting friends, sitting in a coffee house, or resting at his country estate. The "transition from personal to functional management" has not yet taken place here. [5]

Under these conditions, the impact of personality on management is perhaps even stronger than in the more advanced countries. The manager is expected to behave in line with established customs, for example, not to try to force a quick decision on prices or production when it is customary to delay formal decisions for a while even when there is no disagreement. He must have considerable self-confidence in order to pursue a definite course of action in the midst of pressures and delays. The need for a feeling of self-assurance is further accentuated by the lack of precedent which characterizes managerial situations in newly modernizing countries.

My investigations in Latin America showed that the managers themselves widely regarded personal characteristics as even more important than technical and organizational knowledge, which was usually taken for granted. Among desirable personal characteristics, managers mentioned with especial frequency "character," sound family background, the ability to get along with people, and the ability to make decisions and to guide others in a nonauthoritarian manner. Education, initiative, ambition, and enthusiasm for innovation were also mentioned, but not as often.

When the satisfactions and discontents of Latin American managers were explored, personal factors emerged as very important. Among the satisfactions, doing the managerial job itself (including the fulfillment of a creative urge or service to the community), meeting a challenge successfully, and having good relations with associates were the factors most frequently mentioned — far more so than personal income and company profits (which perhaps were taken for granted). Among the discontents, personal and family factors were also quoted frequently, as were small markets, lack of efficiency, and, less frequently, public criticism, state intervention, and trade unions.

Competition is in a special category. The abstract principle of competition is usually approved, sometimes enthusiastically, and it is associated with efficiency and progress even where the economic role of the government is also regarded as essential. But when it comes to the evaluation of competition in the manager's own field of enterprise, only a few, especially self-confident persons, react favorably. Very many take refuge in statements about the poverty of the country, the smallness of the market, the head start of other nations, or the ruthlessness of their own fellow businessmen, in order to show why monopolies, restrictive agreements, tariffs, or public subsidies are required. Competitive innovation is especially rare. Even in new enterprises, at best the managers assume that it is their task to capture an already existing market, especially for goods that have long been imported.

Management Attitudes Toward Labor

In less developed countries, the attitudes of managers toward their workers (who usually came from rural backgrounds) have been, somewhat in the feudal tradition, both exploitative and paternalistic. Workers have been regarded as inferior, primitive beings who owed their economic subsistence to the boss and should, therefore, be at his disposal at all times. Since they really were not worth much to him and could easily be replaced, they were expected to gratefully accept whatever pay he chose to offer, often in kind.

At the same time, the chief considered himself a fatherly mentor and supervisor of these immature beings. At least, he tended to think that *they* considered him a kind of father. No trade union agitators were going to be allowed to stir up these children and destroy their innocence; "papa" employer knew far better what was good for them than they did themselves, and he alone was going to decide on the persons to be promoted.

Times have been changing in this respect, but substantial vestiges of the exploitative and paternalist attitudes remain, and they are sometimes even stronger among the parvenus than among the old upper classes. The degree to which this is true differs greatly according to the country. Within South America, it appears to be far greater in the "Indian" than in the "European" countries, but there are also considerable differences even within the same country.

In some countries, many managers are wishfully convinced that the workers either do, or would like to, view them as fathers if only the trade union leaders and radicals let them. Often welfare institutions of the company are thought to successfully take the place of more old-fashioned forms of paternalism. Elsewhere, managers are equally convinced that the present generation of workers inevitably considers them enemies. Conversely, one can find in some quarters an almost magic belief in "human relations" techniques on American lines as the key to mutual conciliation.

Managers in modernizing countries usually view the attitude of workers toward productivity as lacking in economic understanding or as being outright hostile, but there are some examples to the contrary. As a rule, managers feel that the workers just follow their leaders in labor unions or radical groups. These leaders, in turn, are thought to be driven by lust for power and financial advantages, rather than by civic responsibility.

Other managers point out the casual work habits that are rooted in the cultural traditions of their countries, or trace low productivity to deficient education. But often they are not interested in giving their workers better training for fear that they will subsequently expect higher wages or go elsewhere. There are exceptions to these attitudes in some countries. Many managers feel that

101

it is relatively easy to *make* the worker understand that higher productivity is in his own interest.

Such understanding of productivity, however, is by no means general among the managers themselves. "[In] industrial enterprises managed by former merchants, the efforts of management are generally oriented toward taking advantage of short-run market situations, regardless of production schedules."[6] Quite a few do not know the difference between production and productivity, interpret the latter in a purely technological way, or believe that a drive for higher productivity is pointless in their country because of the smallness of the domestic market and the irremediable competitive advantage of more advanced countries. Others confine themselves to stressing the difficulties which come not only from labor but from bureaucracy, taxation, inflation, and political favoritism. Many hesitate to exchange information. Internal management controls, such as budgeting, costing and financial accounting, and materials control, are still fairly rare and are not fed back systematically into the operations of the enterprise itself. [7]

With such uncertainty within the managerial ranks themselves about the meaning and prospects of higher productivity, their criticism of labor on *this* ground is limited. Generally, criticism of labor is more widespread on the ground of social radicalism, although there is a minority group of managers in many modernizing countries which sympathizes with such ideologies. This social radicalism influences considerably the atmosphere in which managers operate. Their earnings are often quite high in relation to the low income level of their countries and, at times, in relation to managerial incomes in advanced areas, too; but they can never feel certain how long their earnings, their enterprises, and they, themselves, will last. This atmosphere of social radicalism is often mentioned as one reason why long-range planning is impossible in management.

However, there is relatively little worry among managers in the less developed countries about protest movements against economic innovations, especially against industrialization. Destruction of labor-saving machines is not what managers in modernizing countries are likely to fear. Clark Kerr and his associates were right in saying that "[the] protest of today is more in favor of industrialization than against it." [8] But protest movements easily center around the social and economic *effects* of industrialization: Unemployment, slums on the fringe of the new urban and industrial

102

centers, disruption of family life and old customs, and hazards to health and safety in industrial occupations. Rigid refusal of managers to listen to these complaints is not infrequent, nor is the interpretation of any complaints as demagoguery. But there are also some cases of managers sympathizing with such complaints and movements, trying to set an individual example by improving things on the plant level, or attempting to educate their colleagues in human relations and welfare policies in accordance with the practices of wealthier countries (sometimes uncritically).

Management, Inflation, and Foreign Investment

Managerial attitudes toward financial problems in modernizing countries are centered around the shortage of credit and capital, inflationary experiences and dangers, and the role of foreign investment.

The shortage of credit is a common object of complaint, sometimes focused on high interest rates or the virtual impossibility of obtaining business credit at almost any rate. The interpretation of this difficulty varies; some consider it an inevitable trait of less developed economies, while others tend to blame it on specific policies of the government or the banks. But in any case, the conclusion drawn is that extremely high profits are necessary to finance the operations and, especially, since there is practically no other source available, for the expansion of enterprises out of retained profits. This belief is also applied to long-range capital financing, to the limited extent that long-range considerations exist.

Some of this thinking undoubtedly represents a rationalization, for the proportion of high profits that is actually plowed back into the enterprises is quite uneven. At any rate, the perceived capital shortage (as well as credit shortage) undoubtedly colors the entire range of managerial attitudes toward finance. Occasionally, but not very often, it is suggested that part of this much-discussed capital shortage actually reflects wasteful use of the capital that *is* available; for example, through speculative purchases of stocks, foreign exchange, or raw materials, false handling of inventories, or misuse of company funds for personal luxury.

Inflationary experiences and dangers loom large in the financial attitudes of managers. Here again, objective facts and rationalizations blend in one attitudinal structure which often is full of contradictions — both hope and incredulity toward stabilization policies, in particular. On the one hand, inflation is seen as a scourge which makes reliable calculation, long-range planning, and the accumulation of working capital next to impossible, fosters speculative misuse of funds, makes the consumer buy in excess of his real needs, favors the debtor, and forces labor into a constant vain fight for the preservation of its already low standard of living.

On the other hand, inflation is often seen as generating a continuous business boom and, more important, as being the inevitable basis (or consequence) of modernization. A Brazilian industrialist assured me that no one had ever asked him before whether economic development might not be possible *without* inflation! Another one said that inflation would end *after* development has been achieved, just as a millionaire gets respectable once he has made his fortune. There are, however, a few dissenters and also some who simply do not perceive either inflation or modernization in national terms and judge both phenomena according to what their own enterprise gets out of them.

Certainly, inflation is rarely interpreted as the unmixed, devilish evil which it is usually seen to be by managers in more advanced countries. In Brazil, the attitude prevailed for some years that textbook concepts do not really apply to that country because it has got such vast unexploited resources and because its population tends to plow inflationary gains right back into increased production — not into speculation or luxuries. In Argentina, an industrialist said: "People are *born* either inflationists or deflationists, and the group I belong to has an inflationary bias because we feel that there is no economic development without inflation."

Foreign investment also tends to be perceived in an ambivalent way. The emphasis on capital shortage is often linked with a feeling that the only possible source of substantial capital supply for development is foreign investment. In fact, the latter is sometimes presented as a panacea; there are complaints that it is too hesitant to come to modernizing areas, or that public policy does not try systematically enough to attract it.

Belief in the importance of foreign investment, however, is quite often coupled with severe reservations concerning specific arrangements or its actual performance where it has been in operation for some time. [9] Only a limited sector of management in modernizing areas would like to attract foreign investment unconditionally. The most frequent qualification stipulates that foreign investors should not be favored over domestic enterprises, especially potential competitors. Foreigners are welcome to bring in their capital but this should be done on equal terms: for example, without special privileges regarding taxation, tariffs, disposition of profits, or foreign exchange arrangements.

Another school of thought favors foreign investment *if* it is channelled into specific uses. For example, many would like foreign capital to be kept out of basic resources, such as mining and land. The underlying psychological mechanism — the reluctance to part with anything that belongs to one's "own body" — can only be hinted at here. Others would like foreign capital to come in only where no domestic capital is active yet, or where the two would not compete on intrinsically unequal terms. Some would like to confine foreign investment to essential activities or industries. There is also occasional criticism of foreign-owned enterprises draining off the scanty capital resources of the country concerned instead of adding to them, or using imported raw materials for the production of goods for the domestic market. On the other hand, a Colombian businessman commented that "only non-investors can favor government control of investment."

Still another type of qualification of foreign investment concentrates on its specific form. Generally, one of two extremes is favored: Either to have foreign investors lend capital to private or public enterprises in the host country and then to leave them alone, or else to have the foreigners immigrate with their capital, to settle down, and to convert themselves and their capital gradually into *national* assets. The greatest resistance at this point appears to be toward foreign business groups who take financial interest in host-country enterprises only temporarily, do not integrate themselves into the national economy and society, and do attempt to run the show, on the basis of a mentality and set of interests that are alien to the country. Straight portfolio investment over a long period without managerial ambitions is usually considered acceptable but does not arouse much enthusiasm.

The possibilities of international financial collaboration are still perceived by only relatively few managers in modernizing countries. The vision of many is limited by the fact that they tend to perceive problems of insufficient development (or any other socio-economic problems) as pertaining to their particular country or area only. This, of course, is always true up to a certain point. Yet, it is a striking experience to hear certain problems of essentially similar nature expressed in purely national terms when generalizations would be quite justified.

State Intervention and Development Planning

The traditional tendency toward a perception of modernization problems chiefly in national terms is not to be confused with a feeling of national unity, a feeling which in the earlier developmental phases is often quite weak, especially toward other classes up or down the social ladder. The tendency mentioned is closely connected with certain attitudes toward the role of the state in social and economic affairs, especially in development planning. Generally speaking, there is a lack of the strongly emotional anti-state attitude which characterizes the attitudes of American business managers. One reason is that the dividing line between private and public management is often blurred; a private manager of today may have been in the government yesterday and may rejoin it tomorrow.

Complaints about state intervention are usually directed at specific forms, such as unrealistic budgets, excise taxes, political pricing, import and foreign exchange restrictions, or social insurance; or else, at administrative practices, such as red tape, graft, favoritism, slowness, lack of consistency in economic policy, and lack of public incentives for private efficiency. A Uruguayan banker said: "The only part of our economy which is *over*developed is its politics." But government aid may also be interpreted as a *right* of private business and as proof of its power — not the government's. Sometimes there is suspicion of the motives of a specific party in power, rather than criticism of state intervention as such.

Any spirit of laissez-faire is quite rare in modernizing countries. The prevailing attitude toward the state sees the government as an indispensable helper in a modernizing economy; it can do many things wrong, but this does not mean that its help, especially in basic services and capital supply, is not needed. Specific demands for such help — for example, tariff protection — are quite likely to emphasize the needs of a given enterprise or industry and to reject some other methods of intervention, particularly direct state management of enterprises. *Regional* feelings and ambitions remain rather strong, as in Antioquia which likes to consider itself "the Texas of Colombia." Or another example, complaints of being a "forgotten" region are frequent in Rio Grande do Sul where a good many managers feel that São Paulo and Brasilia have been favored unduly.

The feeling of a definite need for public intervention becomes quite strong when the discussion turns to overall development planning. It is a rare manager in these countries who is prepared to leave the modernization of this country entirely to private initiative and competition. This is especially true of industrialization, often seen as the path to real national unity and independence.[10]

It is often pointed out, however, that such planning should not be interpreted as the path to a centralized planned economy on Soviet patterns. What they usually have in mind is a development plan which is based on coordinating and integrating studies and on supervision and encouragement by a public agency, but where the actual conduct of enterprises is left mainly in private hands. However, many managers in modernizing countries are willing to accept direct public ownership (though not always public management) in fields which are basic to the entire economy such as energy, transportation, and social services, and also in fields which cannot hope to attract sufficient capital supply from private sources or do not lend themselves readily to competition in a small and weak economy.

The fundamental question of the *specific* relations between management and the state in the process of modernization remains in most countries without any clear-cut answer. Occasionally there is discussion of the extent to which public policy should concentrate on persuading managers that a given development program is necessary, sound, and in the interest of their enterprises. Another way of formulating this question is to ask in which ways public policy could best *foster* a favorable attitude and, more importantly, the active participation of the managerial group in development planning and modernization. Can such encouragement be achieved best through financial incentives, such as guaranteed prices, depreciation allowances or tax privileges for reinvestment purposes, or should it rely chiefly on moral persuasion and an appeal to patriotic loyalty? To the limited extent that such questions are asked, the answers are contradictory or variable.

Conclusions

Managerial attitudes in modernizing countries should not necessarily be expected to duplicate the mentality of managers in industrialized countries. Potentially, the very fact that in a technical sense management can now draw on the historical experiences of others while adjusting them to local needs, can speed up its knowledge and processes. At the same time, unnecessary or premature

107

destruction of older patterns of business administration before a population is ready for management in the modern sense may arouse resistance, thus slowing down the developmental processes it was meant to speed up.

The application of the historical experiences of others is limited by the cultural setting, as well as the modernization phase of each country. There cannot be, therefore, a body of general rules for public policy on management, which would be applicable in every modernizing country without major adjustments. Many training techniques, it is true, have wide international applications; but the essence of management consists in the organization and direction of specific kinds of *people* in their working processes.

Rules of managerial behavior and incentives that are elaborated for a given country and culture should be applicable to the managers of private, public, and cooperative enterprises. In these countries the borderline between ownership types is often vague; managers may shift from one type of firm to another at any time, and the differences in attitude toward efficiency, labor, and above all, toward the socio-economic needs of the country are not likely to follow along the lines of property systems.

In the course of modernization a transition to *professional management* is likely to occur. The family enterprise clearly cannot be done away with overnight, nor is it necessarily incompatible with professional management. But family connections or prestige should be considered a suitable basis of managerial selection only when those selected also have the training, knowledge, and mentality required for the making of an effective manager. Needless to say, a government which itself is based on nepotism would have a hard time in persuading management to carry out more lofty principles of selection and action.

Delegation of responsibilities, division of labor, and clearly defined functions among executives of the larger enterprises, along with flexibility within the total administrative structure of the enterprise should represent frequent goals of public policy. Another goal is the principle that the efficiency and social utility of the enterprise, rather than the status and prestige of a family, should be the principal guidepost of managerial action.

Prestige considerations need to be toned down in specific decisions about the selection and location of early industries within an essentially agricultural economy. The training of farm managers and the general interpretation of agriculture and of industries that are based on it as promising features of a development plan, are of great importance.

108

Traditional *limitations of production and distribution* in a less developed economy are not necessarily there forever. This applies especially to conscious or unconscious assumptions about a "dual economy" which permanently excludes large sectors of the population from the national market. It also applies to the corresponding neglect of a drive for higher productivity, lower prices, and increasing consumer satisfaction in general. Likewise, the belief that competition represents a luxury which a modernizing economy can never afford, invites serious rethinking among the managers both of private and public enterprise.

It is equally important to encourage long-range managerial planning (and to discourage the association of managerial activity with a constant drive for immediate profit). Such encouragement can be carried out through the coordination of social services, such as road building and housing, long-range investment plans of individual enterprises, public capital supply for private long-range investment integrated into the modernization program, and a general drive for stability in monetary and industrial relations. This can be combined with an attempt to make every manager understand that he cannot carry out his function without taking *some* risks most of the time.

The impact of *personality* on managerial effectiveness is enormous and all that public policy can do is to reward a fine, actual performance through an array of possible measures, ranging from cash to decorations. The most effective reward in more than one culture appears to be the *personal* satisfaction from a job well done.

In the relations between *management and labor*, the exploitative or paternalist attitude of managers can be discouraged by public policy, including social legislation. Both moral and financial incentives for higher productivity to workers, peasants, and managers can be provided. The casual work habits of many populations cannot be changed overnight, and no such attempt will be promising if it clashes head-on with established cultural values. Yet gradual change in these values through the conscious use of education and moral and financial incentives is not impossible.

Such an attempt, as a rule, will be most hopeful if it is carried out by a government which enjoys the confidence of the major population groups. Social radicalism can often be channeled into production attitudes and into support for a national drive for modernization as was shown in chapter 2.

Real *shortages of capital* should not be allowed to be compounded by wasteful use of the available capital, and the for-mation and productive use of capital should be encouraged by such measures as incentive taxation. Such measures, it is true, may be impossible or ineffective if they follow prolonged inflationary experiences. On the other hand, it must be made clear that fear of inflation is not an acceptable permanent excuse for lack of long-range planning or of efficient use of capital in either private or public enterprises.

As for *foreign investment*, there is need everywhere for govern-ments and nations to decide what they really want. They cannot go on crying for foreign capital and then complain about imperial-ism when it comes; they cannot attract it one day and nationalize it the next, nor feel obligated to emulate such practices when carried out by other countries. Candor and clarity on the part of public authorities will encourage a comparable clearing of minds among the managers of domestic enterprises toward any possi-bilities of foreign capital participation.

Managers of foreign-controlled enterprises, at the same time, must also beware of economic schizophrenia. If they are foreigners, they should realize that they cannot expect to live and work in another country forever without fully adjusting themselves to it sooner or later. Unless they come just for a short while as tech-nical advisers, they should make up their minds within two or three years whether they want to stay there for good and become citizens of their new country, or whether they prefer to return to their homeland.

The foreign investor should also understand that no country in our period can let others permanently own a large part of its economy. Public policy should clearly decide whether it wishes to solicit foreign loans without any managerial responsibility on the part of the lenders; straight portfolio investment for a limited number of years; equity investment with or without managerial participation (which is essentially meant to remain in the country along with its profits); international business ventures with joint management; or any other form. One thing is clear from postwar experience: Foreign investment along the old lines, with constant export of the profits and perhaps with permanent foreign manage-ment which never integrates into national life, has increasingly poorer prospects.

The rapidly rising nationalism in modernizing areas can be chan-neled into a systematic effort for constructive development plan-ning. In this endeavor, public policy needs, in the first place, to

110

supply a flow of reliable economic data. It also needs to determine the specific forms in which the collaboration of managerial and other groups, within the general situation of a coordinated modernization, is to be brought about. The "sane" approaches to socio-economic change require some more specific discussion; this will be offered in the following chapter.

CHAPTER 6

Society, Mental Health, and Development Stage[1]

Can the modernizing nations hope to achieve a "healthy and happy" civilization *after* many of the basic economic and technological problems of society have been solved, through developmental processes, as they have been in industrialized countries? Despite the age-old complaints that mankind so easily behaves in a "crazy" way, in economic situations no less than in others and in rich countries no less than poor, the integrated consideration of the socio-economic and psychological aspects of human behavior is fairly new and incomplete. It is only recently that psychology and psychiatry (originally disciplines concerned with the individual) have begun to take social, especially economic, factors into serious consideration.

In economics, the systematic introduction of psychological approaches is of recent date and that of psychiatric elements even more so. But a number of economists now include, in their analysis of such problems as modernization, "irrational" as well as "rational" behavior — the latter usually associated with actions perceived as enhancing self-interest — and some psychiatrists have discovered socio-economic variables in individual psychopathological phenomena. It is the purpose of this chapter to discuss some important points of contact between the two fields of study and their impact on our understanding of developmental processes in society.

Culture, Socio-Economic System, and Personality Formation

The links between the specific culture into which an individual is born and his typical personality formation have been widely studied. For the purposes of this discussion, these links are of special importance because of the extensive economic content of the integrational systems that characterize most cultures. This content includes the level of material well-being, the techniques of production, attitudes toward work, economic status, financial requirements in family life, and the economic role of women.

In some industrialized societies, the economic content of a specific culture has been obscured not merely by the limitations of perception that so often characterize people's reactions toward cultural values, but also by the additional reluctance of society to view its economic arrangements realistically. Nearly every person is emotionally involved in the economic structure through a vested interest either in its maintenance or in its change. Scholarly studies of such problems may also be suspected, rightly or wrongly, because of the scholar's personal preconceptions.

Freud, in whose theoretical system economic factors are all but nonexistent (his "economics of the personality" bears a purely semantic resemblance to the problem before us), unwittingly contributed his share to this situation. Yet, Freud's own concept of man was colored by the economic society around him. "Freud always considers the individual in his relation to others. These relations as Freud sees them, however, are similar to the economic relations to others which are characteristic of the individual in capitalist society. Each person works for himself, individualistically, at his own risk, and not primarily in cooperation with others." [2]

Actually, the conflicts in which individuals find themselves involved during their lifetime are to a large extent conflicts with the demands that their culture imposes on them. These demands are very different from one culture to another, but almost invariably are rich in economic content. This content may be focused on man's working performance (e.g., "he who does not work shall not eat"), on his consumption habits (thrift, or generosity), or on his competitive or cooperative virtues.

Much attention has been paid to the superior mental health of the Hutterite sect in western North America; it lives in simple agrarian communities, owns all property in common, and rears children over two-and-a-half years in common kindergartens where they are socialized chiefly by other children.[3] Mental disorders among Hutterites are quite rare.

If more such studies of the relationship between cultural and socio-economic structure and the state of mental health were available, more definite statements could be made about the extent to which the spread of mental disorders, especially neuroses, in either rich or poor countries can be explained from either cultural or socio-economic factors. If neurosis is an internalized conflict between ego and superego, is not the specific quality of the latter of necessity a basic factor in the frequency and form of neuroses? If the demands of economic society upon the individual emphasize respect for, or veneration of, material property, while simultaneously his religion emphasizes an opposed value system, he may be caught in a conflict which will make him a rebel, a neurotic, or both. Freud minimizes such situations by claiming that abolition of private property would merely deprive aggressiveness of one of its tools without changing the underlying need for personal assertion.[4] But the strength of aggressivity itself in many individuals may, in part at least, be due precisely to the emphasis which a given culture and economic society gives to aggressive attitudes in the course of the socialization process.[5]

The problem has been stated in somewhat different terms by those who have asked whether in the case of a pathological conflict between individual and society, we can always assume that it is the latter which is sane. Halliday raised this question in investigating socio-economic conditions among British miners, conditions which in his opinion were morbid and thus tended to breed psychic, especially psychosomatic, disorders.[6] Fromm broadened the problem area as follows:

> The concept of mental health depends on our concept of the nature of man ... The needs and passions of man stem from the peculiar condition of this existence.... An unhealthy society is one which creates mutual hostility, distrust, which transforms man into an instrument of use and exploitation for others, which deprives him of a sense of self, except inasmuch as he submits to others or becomes an automaton ... Freud's concept of human nature as being essentially competitive (and asocial) is the same as we find it in most authors who believe that the characteristics of man in modern Capitalism are his natural characteristics.[7]

Fromm points to certain traits in the social character of the capitalist, industrialized period, such as "alienation" affecting workers and managers, owners and consumers; bureaucratization; separation of wealth from spiritual values; the alienating function of

114

money; the tendency toward obsessive work; and the feeling of helplessness toward economic and social forces.

The approach that sees sanity as a problem for society, no less than for the individual, is generally valid but can easily be overdone. Many who would go along with Fromm find themselves at odds with that other socio-economic interpretation of mental disorders, the one supplied by Marxism in its strange Soviet Russian variety. With some fluctuations, the Soviet concept of man has been materialist and deterministic. This has sometimes meant chiefly the determination of man's development by his social environment; in other cases, it has emphasized the environment being shaped by men's social action. At the same time, man has been thought of as a conscious, rational and purposive being who is fully responsible for his actions.

The psychiatric application of these Soviet ideas about man has led to a curious attempt to combine Marxian dialectics with a revival of Pavlov's theory of conditioned reflexes. Consciousness is seen as the reflection of social existence in the human mind. It is only the class division and exploitation of capitalist society that produce mental disorders, especially neuroses. Mental disorders, at the same time, have been thought to represent either a function of a particular economic class situation or the effect of physiological anomalies (e.g., of the nervous system, although almost any belief in the role of hereditary factors has been frowned upon). Psychoanalysis has been considered "erroneous" partly because of its individualist character and partly because of its emphasis on unconscious factors. The continued occurrence of mental disorders, crime and alcoholism in the Soviet Union has been explained by the survival of remnants of capitalist consciousness — not a very impressive argument more than half a century after the Bolshevik revolution — or possibly by war injuries. Soviet psychotherapy has emphasized persuasion and education, suggestion and hypnosis, and changes in the social environment such as work therapy, including forced labor. However, Soviet life itself has been thought of as psycho-therapeutic in its emphasis on collective interests over egotistic ones. [8]

Soviet Russia thus provides a warning of possible socio-economic scotomata to psychiatrists and economists everywhere. A social and economic philosophy based on the premise that the human mind is molded by economic factors seemed to promise revealing studies about psycho-economic problems in Soviet Russia's own society. Instead, the Russians developed a defensive

115

mechanism of denial both of many economic problems and of their interaction with mental health. This happened in a country that might well have studied the psychiatric effects of hunger epidemics in the twenties, of the mentality of forced-labor camps, of revolutionary changes in the status and work performance of the peasant, of forcible disruption of families, and the mental and economic pressure of a totalitarian apparatus. For countries where science is thought of as free and independent, this example offers a warning to be on the lookout for possible blind spots at home.

Even though Soviet Marxism holds little promise in supplying a foolproof theoretical basis for the integration of economic and psychiatric concepts, the idea of a psychologically healthy society is real, and it poses itself with special emphasis in the modernizing societies today. The nineteenth century thought it had found the answer in emphasizing "rationality." In the meantime, this criterion has not only become less precise but has also come to assume quite different meanings in psychology and in economics. In psychology the concept of rationality has been related to prevailing or required patterns of attitudes and behavior in a given culture and society, and has been considered a matter of degree, rather than an absolute that either does or does not exist in a given individual. Likewise, in economics, rationality has become a more relative concept than before and has, in addition, increasingly been given the meaning of a purely hypothetical or normative assumption of choice patterns for methodological purposes, rather than meaning the behavioral characteristics of an existing economic man.

The decline of the rationality criterion, however, has left us with the question of which kinds of personality promise economic success in a given society, and which methods of psychotherapy can help certain individuals to increase their economic effectiveness (not necessarily in the popular sense of "getting rich quick"). A detailed discussion of the personality traits that are conducive to economic effectiveness under changing socio-cultural requirements (for example, certain types of time perspective, thrift, initiative, daring or organizational ability) would exceed the scope of this chapter.

It is sufficient to mention here that the specific requirements of economic effectiveness vary enormously with culture, social order and development stage, and the prevailing economic philosophy. Psychiatric removal of unconscious barriers to thrift, for instance, might have done a person far more good in an early Puritan capitalism than in a late twentieth century industrialized economy of relative abundance. In one kind of culture or socio-economic order, work will be regarded as punishment, in another kind as pleasure; aggressiveness, competitiveness, single-mindedness, co-operativeness will receive economic rewards in one society and lead to personal disaster in another. There has been considerable variation in the economic characteristics in an individual that are considered normal or rational and, correspondingly, in the fre-quency of behavior in economic situations that is classified as nonrational. Moreover, certain economic societies may choose to reward nonproductive orientations, in Fromm's terms, such as an exploitative or hoarding orientation, and may consider a produc-tive orientation abnormal.

Economic Conditions and the Family Situation

Among the socio-economic influences that help to shape an individual's personality either in a "normal" or an "abnormal" direction, family environment stands out as probably the most important. In fact, psychoanalytic interpretations of personality formation have tended to consider almost exclusively the in-fluence of parents and siblings upon a child.

Now it could be argued that everybody in the world is not reared by his parents. In fact, there are societies where children typically are *not* reared by their parents. In early Israeli Kibbutzim, a professional nurse often replaced mother and father to a large extent for *every* child in the community; there were few intensive sibling relations; women had no individual housework and men no individual business or job worries. Whatever the group effects of this arrangement may have been, it exemplified a nonfamily type of child-rearing.

For the purposes of this discussion, however, we can assume that child-rearing by the family is the rule among most popula-tions, and that such early childhood influences have a very impor-tant impact on personality formation. The question that concerns us next is to what extent this family situation reflects socio-economic conditions and development stages.

A realistic appraisal of the parents' influence on a child's per-sonality must allow for the fact that parents not only range from authoritarian and rigid to understanding and loving, but also have an essential role in the family as providers in most societies. When-

117

ever this economic role (or the coherence of the family in general) is disturbed by deprivation, unemployment, bankruptcy, inflation or simply general lack of economic stability, important effects on the role of the parents are likely to result. The unemployment situation in industrialized societies, in which mother may go to work while father stays at home, thus reversing their usual roles toward the children, has been extensively studied by Mirra Komarovski and others. Further economic problems that frequently face families in the poorer classes of industrialized (and, for that matter, of newly modernizing) societies are excessive working hours of father and/or mother, the constant threat of changes in jobs and residence, and barriers to social advancement. This does not mean, of course, that economic influences on the family situation are confined to the poorer classes; in the upper groups, the "busy" father who has little time for the children, the socialite mother, expectation of inheritance, or an atmosphere of constant concentration on money-making and spending to the detriment of other values, may deeply influence the relations between parents and children, or between siblings.

In other words, economic determinants of the family situation exist in all the socio-economic groups, though not in the same ways. The great economic vulnerability of the family with children is inevitably of great importance for the family situation in economically advanced societies.[9] Many a child is consciously or (more often) unconsciously imbued, perhaps through casual remarks of other family members, with the feeling that he was really an unwanted burden, and he may develop guilt feelings on this ground. The change in the economic role of women in an industrial society, with constant pressure to take or keep a job, has led to partial loss of the mother's role. This is not altered by the fact that the chief incentive for women to work is not always financial; often, it is precisely the desire to get away from the confines of homemaking and to improve their social status. The psychological effects of a woman's work on her children are of considerable importance.[10]

Changes in technology and living patterns have affected family relations in industrial societies. Television has brought the image of "TV dinners" to many children whose parents cannot afford such dinners, and has made small but powerful high-pressure salesmen (without commission) out of children whose parents may despise what is advertised. Thousands of families moved out of deteriorating city districts into the suburbs only to find that the commuting father has even less time for the children than before, and that mother may feel rootless in the new community.[11] Other effects of such changes have, of course, been more favorable.

This is not the place to discuss biological factors in mental diseases, but economic conditions often affect the *general* state of health in some or all families in a given society. Economic conditions that are reflected in intellectual and emotional development can determine to a great extent the choice of mate, use of contraception, the number of desired children, and the use of a physician's advice and help. Unhealthy housing or working conditions may help produce sickly parents, or wear out the life energies of basically healthy parents long before the children have grown up. All this is not meant to assert that the economics of family life determines its content entirely. There are other influences (such as ethnic and religious), but many insights have been gained by looking into the economic condition in the family in which a psychiatric patient was reared, and in some cases by shaping a family therapy accordingly.[12] A patient's elaboration of economic problems may conceal deeper needs, but in cases where the patient never mentions such problems at all, the psychotherapist may by accepting such silence unwittingly contribute to a denial of economic realities.

Mental Health and Work Performance

The fact than an individual's personality and state of mental health have an important influence on his work performance may be self-evident to psychologists, but this fact has received relatively little attention in applied economics which has usually interpreted work in terms of "disutility," rather than in terms of the individual's activity, drive, and place in society. Specifically, emotional factors (especially unconscious influences) are very important in decisions about occupational choice and in turning this initial choice into success or failure. For the economist, this is especially important from the viewpoint of effective utilization of human resources and the prevention of large-scale waste of manpower, a problem of great significance in modernizing societies.[13]

Conversely, the psychotherapist is interested in unsatisfactory occupational situations, including lagging community adjustment in industry, which may encourage neurotic and anti-social behavior, psychosomatic disturbances, and other clinical phenomena.

119

The steadily increasing number of older persons who respond unfavourably to the loss of old community relations and social roles — a loss that is often the effect of aimless retirement — has been adding to the tasks of the psychotherapist. In other cases, great differences in the occupational and financial situations of old parents and their children have resulted in difficulties. Another occupational situation the psychotherapist is up against with increasing awareness concerns the employment handicaps of former mental patients in their relations both with employers and with fellow workers, especially in a "soft" labor market.

In meeting such tasks, industrial society has sometimes been hampered by certain Freudian interpretations of the role of work in human life. Freud says that work integrates an individual into the community and social reality; but he adds that "the great majority of people work only out of necessity, and in this natural human aversion to work the most difficult social problems are rooted."[14] We need not go to the other extreme of assuming an "instinct of workmanship" in order to question the existence of such a "natural aversion."

Nevertheless, work relations in industrialized societies frequently do result in a psychiatric problem, usually of the neurotic type. The most obvious form of this problem is presented by occupational neuroses. Neurotic symptoms may occur after minor industrial accidents in individuals with a background of failings and inadequacies, whose strong dependency needs are unable to resist the temptation afforded by the accident. "Rewarding such precipitated neurotic symptoms with financial gain may aggravate the condition."[15] In addition to accident-proneness, absenteeism in factories has been found to be due in a substantial degree to neurotic conditions. Job changes can also be caused by such conditions; and also, job change due to external factors may touch off a variety of latent psychic disturbances even when the change involves a promotion. There is some evidence of occupational psychoses which various authors believe to be inversely related to income and prestige.[16] Night work has been found to affect family and sex life, and to require both psychological and physiological adjustments which are easier for some than for others.

Psychiatric disability need not mean occupational disability. Industrial psychiatry, which traditionally has concentrated on aptitude tests, monotony, and reduction of fatigue, apparently has changed its emphasis and is now paying greater attention to the problem of channelling existing neurotic potentials into productive performance both in a direct and an indirect sense of the word. The use of psychiatrists or psychologists by companies in order to evaluate foremen and executives is fairly frequent now.

The neurotic or emotionally unstable person in an executive position represents a problem of special importance (which was touched upon in chapter 4). It is rather doubtful whether executive pressures as such — either competition within the corporate hierarchy or the more general pressures of social climbing — cause disturbances where no such potential exists already; but there is little doubt that neurotic persons in executive positions tend not to delegate responsibilities, to be unstable or unclear in their decisions, to be torn by conflicting desires for dependence and independence, to be authoritarian or paternalistic, and to antagonize colleagues or employees in many ways. Similar tendencies of course, may be seen in labor union officers with comparable personality traits and emotional needs.

Class Situation and Mental Disorder

The ecology of mental disorders has made great progress in recent years and is more often focused now on socio-economic differences in the pattern of disorders. However, once we attempt to break down the published general data, from such sources as the National Association for Mental Health, according to socio-economic groups and the types of disorders, we get on thin ice. It is not very certain at this point to what extent progressing urbanization — a crucial problem in modernizing societies — is necessarily bringing changes in the patterns of illness. One study from the United States concluded that "urban individuals have higher rates of mental illness in that rural illness seems to be most commonly a manifestation of guilt and disturbance in social feelings, whereas mental illness in city populations seems to be related to competitive, highly ambitious, and compulsive living patterns." [17]

The now famous study by Faris and Dunham in the thirties came to the conclusion that psychoses show a regular decrease from the center to the periphery of cities, and that each disorder has a characteristic distribution within the city (with paranoia, for example, concentrated in hotel and rooming house districts and the highest incidence of schizophrenia found in slum areas); but this study offered no convincing causal explanation of the pattern found. [18]

For our purposes, a more important question concerns the socio-economic distribution of mental disorders.[19] There is some evidence that the incidence of neuroses in industrial societies is higher in the upper occupational and income groups than in the lower, while the figures for psychoses point the opposite way. The trail-blazing study by Hollingshead and Redlich on mental disorders in New Haven, U.S.A., expanded the problem and approach considerably, even though its concept of class omitted the income factor.[20] This study attempted to show that: (1) the prevalence of treated mental illness was related significantly to an individual's position in the class structure; (2) the types of diagnosed psychiatric disorders were connected significantly with the class structure; (3) the kind of psychiatric treatment administered by psychiatrists was associated with the patient's position in the class structure; (4) social psychodynamic factors in the development of psychiatric disorders were correlative to an individual's position in the class structure; (5) mobility in the class structure was associated with the development of psychiatric difficulties.

Specifically, Hollingshead and Redlich showed that a definite association exists between class position and being a psychiatric patient, and that the lower the class the greater was the proportion of patients in the population. Another interesting finding concerned the extent to which the attitudes of everybody concerned toward mental illness varied with socio-economic status — the attitudes of the psychiatrist, the family, and the patient himself.

A more recent study of the social distribution of schizophrenia, which tried to integrate the findings of many earlier investigations, came to the conclusion that "schizophrenic behavior is concentrated in the lowest social stratum due to (1) the processes of socialization which result in a considerable number of individuals with poor cognitive abilities to structure reality, and (2) the requirement of interaction with an unstructured, ambiguous, and punitive reality. Schizophrenic behavior may be regarded as the 'meshing' of these two components."[21]

Assuming then, that the incidence and distribution of mental disorders in industrial societies are related in some ways to socio-economic position, the major theoretical question remains of how this occurs, to the extent at least that this differential is not rooted in purely biological or physiological differences between classes. Many neurotic disorders in some industrialized societies cannot fully be understood without reference to a prevailing system of socio-economic values which places emphasis on success in the material sense and assumes that financial failure indicates personal inadequacy. Such a value system not only virtually forces members of the lower economic groups into "inferiority complexes" — unless they make up for this pressure by "solidarity feelings" — but also imposes a heavy potential handicap on members of the upper groups who are constantly faced with the threat of individual failure in a dynamic society. In J. Ruesch's formulation, "flexibility and social change are in America the principal sources of insecurity, while in Europe stratification and rigidity result in frustration." [22] External adversities such as business failure, even in an objectively declining market, can apparently be a predisposing factor in paranoid behavior (J.S. Tyhurst). [23]

The value system concerned considers the businessman as a social ideal or leader. It regards competition as intrinsically good and socially useful; money and property are considered the yardstick and symbol of success in the competitive tournament. The knight in shining armor is thought to be the one who has won the most money, although in earlier phases of capitalism, a moneyed leisure class based on inheritance had an equally high if not superior standing.

The "belief" in money is uneasy, however, and is increasingly modified in corporate hierarchies by other aims such as personal and company prestige, maintenance of production and employment, and long-range expansion goals; but money retains much of its symbolic character within the explicit value system of industrialized countries. Often the drive for money symbolizes sublimated libidinous pleasures. Psychotherapists are familiar with overt money drives which are basically related to an individual's sex and love needs. A clinical investigation in Germany of the psychic elements in money and property behavior showed that psychiatric patients were very adversely affected by being deprived of such personal property as wedding rings, and also that those patients whose perception and memory still functioned adequately did not behave differently in money matters (such as payment habits and trust in paper money) from a matched sample of "normal" persons. [24] Those mental patients whose disturbance expresses itself largely in "abnormal" economic behavior are quite likely to attribute almost magic powers to money.

Another aspect of socio-economic class structure and values is the prevalence of class guilt feelings both in the lower and upper income groups of industrial society. The lower groups are often plagued by the implied inferiority of those who were either born poor or had failed in their attempts to acquire money later. Those sections of the lower groups that belong to racial, ethnic or religious minorities are particularly exposed to adverse valuations by others and potentially by themselves.[25] The upper groups also have their share of class guilt feelings. They feel responsible, primarily on the unconscious level, for the misery of the underprivileged at home and abroad, or for other economic shortcomings of "their" society, such as unemployment, slums or inflation. Moreover, they are exposed to the threat of losing their favored position within a constantly changing society. Guilt or inferiority feelings (not to be confused with genuine social responsibility) often prevent the enjoyment of leisure by people who could easily afford it.

Finally, the class situation of mental patients has been found to have a very important bearing on the therapy they receive. It has often been pointed out that Freud's theories had their origin in the social environment of upper middle class Viennese during the Imperial period. More important, the socio-economic background of a patient is likely to influence a person's relative receptiveness to psychotherapy in general or to a specific kind of treatment, including medication.[26]

The patterns of diagnosis and treatment depend in a large degree on the patient's class, if the New Haven findings of Hollingshead and Redlich are generally applicable. These authors found that "psychotherapeutic method and particularly insight therapy are applied in disproportionately high degrees to higher status neurotic patients being treated by private practitioners," while most patients in the poorer groups receive organic therapy for the same disorders (and various others). Value differences between high-status psychiatrist and lower-status patients were found to be a serious obstacle in psychotherapy. We cannot assume that there is one medical pattern in existence for the treatment of a given disorder that is valid without reference to the socio-economic status of the patient.

Economic Fluctuations and Mental Disorders

Have the periodic fluctuations that have characterized economic life in industrial capitalistic countries since the early nineteenth century been related to collective ups and downs in the psychic condition of individuals? If so, in what way? This is a very complex

124

question to which a full answer is not yet available, and all we can do here is to outline its various aspects.

From the economist's point of view, business "cycles" have not been really cyclical in the sense of strict regularity. The periods involved and the intensity of upswings and downturns have varied. Some industries have always been ahead of others in the process of fluctuation, and a distinction has long been made between overlapping shorter and longer waves of economic fluctuation. Yet, there is little doubt about the recurrent — and by now widely anticipated — character of fluctuations in the economic life of industrialized nations.

The equally well-known fluctuations in the psychic condition of individuals, and in the incidence of specific disturbances — especially neurotic ones — have not as yet been clearly proved either to cause or to be caused by the economic fluctuations mentioned. Shall we conclude that there is no such relationship and that the connection between economic and psychic "depressions," in particular, is purely semantic? Such a conclusion would be excessive.

To begin with, suicide rates *are* related to the phase of the business cycle; they tend to rise during economic slumps and to fall during prosperity, especially among the upper economic groups. Some authors explain this phenomenon in terms of the rise of frustrations and the loss of status and hierarchical ranking which result from economic failure. [27] (Homicide, on the other hand, appears to rise during prosperity.) We cannot here go into the question of whether *all* suicides are to be considered evidence of mental disorder; it suffices to say that this is certainly often true.

The connection between economic and psychic fluctuations, however, is much stronger than this. Working capacity and, with it, the effect of work therapy differ in prosperity and in depression. What differs even more is the social evaluation of working capacity. In the formulation of C. Tietze: "Now, in 1933, of course, a person who didn't hold a job was a deviate. There was something wrong with him. He was shiftless or lazy or incompatible or unadaptable, or what not. . . . In 1936, he was just a victim of circumstances: he was out of work; that was too bad for him, but he wasn't a personality deviate any more, so we had to toss out this whole body of data referring to time comparison." [28]

Shame and guilt feelings of parents toward children may develop over unemployment, deprivation, or bankruptcy. Conversely, children's mental development may be affected by fear

125

that their father might lose his job or his money. Loss of one or the other may be interpreted by people as loss of health or social function, and may otherwise affect adversely their self-esteem. Today, there is still a basic block to mutual understanding between the older generation which has the Great Depression in their bones and the younger generation which has been brought up in an atmosphere of affluence (even if they are not affluent themselves). [29]

The constant threat of fluctuations in the economic situation of each individual, even when the economy as a whole seems reasonably stable, tends to erode the psychic energies of many. Economic competition offers an outlet to individuality and initiative; but it also often constricts the energies of individuals into a narrowly limited pattern of interest and rules of the game, and it imposes severe economic and social sanctions on those who come out of the contest without any great measure of success. Even those who are successful in the economic sense may develop feelings of frustration once they discover that financial success does not necessarily mean personal happiness.

The competitive process in a developed economy, accentuated by periodic economic fluctuations often channels the survival urge, rivalry feelings, assertive needs, and personal aspirations into a single direction that may easily be changed by objective market factors outside the individual's own control. No matter how hard he tries and how ably he arranges his economic matters, he may find that he is still economically run over. He lives in a "fear economy" in which, even as a succesful leader, he remains exposed to status anxiety and threats to his ego from possible economic setbacks. In Horney's words, "competition is a problem for everyone in our culture and it is not at all surprising to find it an unfailing center of neurotic conflicts." [30]

Moreover, the businessman lives in a world that is full of enemies or critics of "his" economic system. His own trade associations flood him with literature crying out against constant threats to free enterprise from a government that he has been conditioned to regard, at least in theory, as dangerous and as his natural enemy.

Certain structural changes in the economy further affect the pattern of life of the successful groups in industrialized countries. The appearance in business of the hired executive who is no longer a controlling owner, and who is part of a complex hierarchic structure within the corporation concerned, has accentuated the imper-

126

sonal or group character of many economic activities. The Organization Man may not necessarily be the morbid figure sometimes described, but he is exposed to enough pressures to make him a fairly frequent candidate for emotional troubles. In the United States *Fortune*, a magazine which addresses itself largely to business executives, has reported these trends in such articles as "Executive Discontent," the "Executive Crack-Up," and so on; *Nation's Business* had, in its May 1968 issue, an article on "Why Successful Businessmen Fail." Similarly, German journals have been frequently discussing *Die Managerkrankheit*, especially its psychosomatic manifestations.

The Economic Cost of Mental Disorders

The magnitude of direct public spending for the treatment of mental disorders, inadequate as it is, represents in the United States an economic problem of sizable proportions.[31] Based on data from the National Institute of Mental Health, a recent study estimated the proportion of those afflicted by mental illness in the United States at about 10 percent and the total cost of mental illness to American society at almost $20 billion for 1966. The financial burden remains enormous despite the slight drop in the patient population of mental hospitals in recent years, a drop possibly due to the use of tranquilizers and new therapeutic processes which have shortened the average length of stay. First admissions are apparently still rising and readmissions even more.

If there is any socio-economic problem in this field that surpasses in impact the over-all figures cited, it is the unequal facilities and treatment, determined by class status, for psychiatric patients inside and outside the mental hospitals. [32] Hollingshead and Redlich found that "expenditures on treatment are linked in highly significant ways with class status in each type of psychiatric facility; the higher-status patient is better off not only in private practice and hospitals but also in the clinics and state hospitals." Thus far, health insurance, whose importance is greatest to the lower income groups, has not included mental disease in its coverage in any adequate way.

A mental block toward the financial aspects of psychic disorders exists in the minds of many legislators in rich countries and presumably, in the minds of the voters who elect them. They do not like being reminded of the spread of mental disease, and their

127

stinginess toward therapeutic and research needs in this field may in itself reveal pathological traits. Little has been done thus far to correct the severe shortage in most countries of psychiatric manpower, including doctors, hospital nurses, psychologists, and psychiatric aides. Expenditures on research, preventive facilities, child guidance, and care of ex-hospital patients have been particularly inadequate.

Perhaps this failure to provide adequate funds for mental health merely reflects a basic social pathology which manifests itself in the frequency of mental disorders coupled with the hestitation of industrial society to do something effective about them. Aside from mental disease in a strict sense, there are various pathological occurrences in society which in many cases are closely related to mental diseases: alcoholism, drug addiction, crime, accidents, suicides. It would be difficult (even if there were conceptual agreement) to specify the share of mental disease in these occurrences, but it is known that there are at least four million problem drinkers including one million severe chronic alcoholics in the United States, and juvenile delinquency has been spreading. It has been estimated that 80 to 90 percent of all accidents are due to psychological (though not always psychiatric) causes. The economic cost of the pathological occurrences mentioned defies calculation, but it must be staggering.

Even this, however, is not the full story of the economic cost of mental disorders in "advanced" societies. The indirect cost due to absenteeism, excessive job mobility, inability to work effectively and consistently, the urge to remain dependent on others, reluctance to work for money, and other emotional impediments results in a constant manpower loss of many millions of man-hours, amounting in the U.S., for example, to billions of dollars lost each year in wages, sales, taxes, and increased rates for private and social insurance. Mental disorders also involve a reduction in life expectancy and, with it, the economic value of the individual.

Last but not least, there is an enormous range of abnormal behavior in economic situations, the financial effects of which can only be guessed at. The person who is possessed of an acute fear of success out of a guilt complex toward his parents, fellow workers, or others offers one example of costly inhibitions. Other examples of abnormal behavior that is economically wasteful include hoarding; gambling; inability to make decisions; fluctuations between depression and manic elation resulting in contradictory actions; paranoid delusions of persecution or grandeur affecting business relations with others; schizoid delusions about imagined market or investment opportunities; hysteric panic-selling or buying; neurotic aversion toward the use of credit as a result of associating debt with guilt; spending compulsions; disturbed interpersonal relations resulting in the inability to get on with employers, employees, customers, or co-workers; uncontrollable aversion to certain modes of transportation, such as subway or airplane; and hypochondriac reaction to insurance.

Every psychotherapist knows such cases of abnormal economic behavior from his practice. In many cases, it is true, he can recognize the pathological motivation of such behavior without knowledge of the real economic situation. Such knowledge, however, *will* be necessary in order to prevent him from making therapeutic mistakes and to enable him to discuss the situation with the patient intelligently. To the extent that his own economic information is derived from contacts with patients, he needs to keep in mind that this information may be warped. A wide and rewarding field of intellectual expansion is open here to psychotherapists. Aside from helping patients to achieve financial rewards, some indirect help may also be supplied in removing obstacles from the economic machinery of industrial society.

Socio-Economic Trends Affecting Mental Health

Certain basic changes in social and economic life which have been under way in recent years have affected, or are affecting, the state of mental health in developed countries, although the exact impact cannot always be evaluated. Some, but not all, of these changes also affect newly modernizing countries in varying degrees.

(a) *The new industrial technology*, resulting in ever greater mechanization and automation of work in many occupations, has changed not only the training but the emotional requirements for workers in factories and offices. Although work has become easier and cleaner in many jobs, its impersonal character and the danger of monotony and fatigue have increased. So has the fear of future unemployment (and with it, of loss of a personal function in society), a fear which persists even in the midst of prosperity. People with a shaky emotional structure of personality, which might have been adequate under slower and more individualized conditions of work, may succumb to the new type of strain. The new skills or reactions required may make some individuals appear inadequate, whose mental equipment might have been sufficient under different conditions of work and life.

Moreover, the military application of recent technological developments such as nuclear energy and rocketry has resulted in a constant feeling in many people of threat to national *and* individual survival. This felt threat may upset the shaky emotional balance of persons who have already had a thin margin of security feeling.

(b) *The increasing life expectancy* of men and, especially, women in the absence of major war action, marks great socioeconomic progress but also raises new psychological problems. We can expect for the future an increase in the number of those disorders which are to some extent correlated with old age. In addition, the failure of many "developed" societies thus far to make adequate provisions for meaningful ways for their citizens to spend their declining years may increase pressures on the mental health of many older people. Even younger age groups find themselves faced, in an economy of relative abundance, with an emotional problem that would have been inconceivable for earlier generations, namely, how to spend the increasing leisure hours in a meaningful and emotionally satisfying way instead of merely killing time, succumbing to the frustrations of boredom, or vainly engaging in pseudo-activities such as watching TV for endless hours or spending one's time at the race track.

(c) *The new economy of abundance*, although far from relieving the economic worries and frustrations of the many remaining poor, has constantly increased the range of goods and services that are readily accessible to the average consumer. It has, however, also cluttered his life with countless gadgets of very limited use and has put him under constant pressure to conform with other consumers, especially those in the same social group.

Moreover, poverty in an indigent economy is psychologically quite different from poverty in an affluent society. Pressure to rise is qualitatively different in a rigid, strongly stratified setting, from such pressure in a more fluid society. In countries like the U.S. with its strong horizontal (geographic) as well as vertical (class) mobility, many problems of socio-economic origin present themselves to the student of personality who delves into individual childhood. For example, the patient who was a child born in poverty sees that the parents, more prosperous by then, give the younger children so much more than he received; this may be seen as lack of love. If the parents get poorer and mother has to go to work, the effects may be similarly interpreted. If father is unemployed for a long time, there is a characteristic reaction of sadness and frustration due to loss of the "omnipotent" provider, plus resentment and hatred, often mixed with greater than usual amounts of guilt feelings. If the rise of the father from poverty and insignificance to abundance and prestige is conspicuous, there is often a strengthening of omnipotence fantasies in children, with a secondary increase in father fixation. If once prosperous parents were impoverished before the children were born, they tend to create confusion in children by promoting the standards, values, and customs of a higher socio-economic class than the one to which they now belong. One of many symptoms is cultivation of the "proper manners" of a higher class, most of which are *not* "proper" in a poorer class environment; or teaching the children sophisticated expressions in an environment where dialect or slang is the established mode of communication.

(d) *Housing shortage.* The perennial scarcity of good housing at moderate rates has affected nearly every nation in the world, rich or poor, and has made it difficult or impossible for a great many individuals to realize the feeling of having a real home. At the same time, many of the new housing developments designed to improve these conditions have failed to lead to the formation of a community that gives the individual a feeling of support and belonging.

Studies of social morbidities due to bad housing, particularly crowding within slum dwellings, have shown that such conditions can have profound effects on personality formation, sex life, and mental health. Sometimes such experiences affect the majority of children in a given area. One study concludes that "the individual shows a marked absence of a strict and efficient conscience, an unwillingness and inability to deal with disturbing or unpleasant situations and a flight from these." He is unable to postpone satisfactions; this leads to negativism, distrust, marked aggressiveness which is permitted violent expression.[33] Middle class families have sought relief from the evils of an urban environment, which offers little to their children, in a new suburbia of one-family houses and backyards. For some of them, the move was successful, but others found that lack of privacy and increased pressures for conformity haunted them in their new habitat. Moreover, the loss of contact with relatives and friends, and long commuting hours, were the price they had to pay for the move. There have been reports of a "suburban neurosis," especially in women, due to a feeling of isolation in the new environment. In other words, neither the economic and financial nor the social and psychological aspects of the housing problem have been fully solved yet, in industrial or newly modernizing societies.

(e) *The aspirations of poverty-stricken populations*, especially the widespread quest for industrialization or general modernization, have suggested to the rich nations a re-examination of their own concepts of psychic functioning and health, in order to avoid ethnocentrism in their international behavior and aid policies. These aspirations have also generated a host of new problems of mental health in the modernizing countries as they undergo basic technological and economic changes.[34] The whole idea of individual psychotherapy, for example, looks absurd when applied to huge populations such as those of India or China, and a public policy for mental health inevitably comes to mind. Other Western concepts also invite re-examination: instead of the broken family, interest may center on the "too closely knit" family of newly modernizing countries, which may have problems when modern industry and its work requirements are introduced. Disruption of the old, "backward" patterns of child-rearing and rural community life in the course of industrialization and urbanization (before people are ready for any new, supposedly superior patterns) may have very detrimental effects and may result in widespread frustration. This, in turn, fosters individual or collective aggressiveness, apathy, alcoholism, drug addiction, gambling and various other attempts at flight from the new, frightening reality. Many of these effects may appear less in those who have been uprooted than in their children. Such social disorganization may also increase the appeal of totalitarian movements and pseudo-solutions in newly modernizing countries, as was pointed out in chapter 2.

Conclusions

The traditional psychophobic inclination of many economists to ignore the functioning of the human mind offers no excuse for the comparable lack of interest on the part of many psychologists in the essential factors and issues of socio-economic life — a blind spot that has resulted largely from a subconscious uneasiness in this group about the implications of these factors and issues. Socio-economic insights may disturb a number of convenient, if conventional, assumptions and rationalizations, and may interfere with the simplified relation that was thought in the past to exist between more or less isolated individuals. Yet, economic knowledge in practicing psychologists could probably increase their therapeutic effectiveness and could help in avoiding possible damage to persons and groups treated, from insufficient understanding of their life experience and setting.

What kinds of socio-economic problems are the most important to know about for this purpose? (1) The economic aspects of cultural change, the nature of the various socio-economic orders and their historical sequence, and the impact of both culture and socio-economic order upon the typical pattern of personality formation in a given society. (2) The class structure of the society concerned, the prevailing standards of personal success, occupational choice and work performance expected, and the share of occupational and other economic conditions in the prevailing pattern of family life. (3) The differences among the value systems of the various socio-economic groups; differences which have often resulted in lack of mutual understanding. (4) Business fluctuations, especially the impact of depressions and inflations upon the family and the individual; the types of unemployment and the role of the money and credit system in employment and business. (5) The impact of changing technology and managerial organization on industrial and clerical work, executive requirements, and consumer preferences. (6) Changing perceptions of business activity and the role of profit on the part of managerial and other groups. (7) The effect of urban growth and housing shortages on people's home life, along with the increase of public welfare policies and economic intervention in general. (8) The differences among nations in the phases and patterns of socio-economic development and modernization, and the conceptual and practical limits of applying a psychological framework from industrialized countries to most populations in Asia, Africa, or Latin America.

Another conclusion concerns the uses and possible misuses of psychological techniques for dubious economic or ideological purposes. Subliminal advertising has aroused the public to the dangers of employing advances in psychology for commercial, and perhaps political, goals. Psychotherapy is in danger of being interpreted by some of its own practitioners as a method of directing patients toward specific economic goals, such as joining father's business or a labor union, no matter what might be the objective merits of such actions in a given case. Even greater care is required to avoid the direction of patients toward a specific socio-economic system, national pattern of modernization, or ideology that is perceived as normal at a given time, and in clearly distinguishing personal adjustment from socio-economic adaptation, let alone conformity.

In other words, the practice of psychology inevitably involves great socio-economic responsibility, a fact which is easily obscured or distorted not only by the person-to-person situation, but also by the fact that the practicing psychologist is ordinarily *paid* for his work. Since prevailing social attitudes toward money in industrial societies tend to associate it not only with success but with guilt, unconscious conflicts may arise from this situation in both doctor and patient. Medical service in general and psychotherapy in particular do not lend themselves too easily to usual financial standards — it is like paying God. The anthropologist, in a sense, is better off: *he* pays his "patient"!

Certain psychotherapists interpret the reluctance of many people to invest large sums of money in treatment as a pathological symptom in itself. Perhaps it *sometimes* is, but the fact remains that in industrial cultures, most people have not only "too little money" but "too little time" (since being busy is often a status device) to undergo lengthy treatment. Some people may quite rationally prefer a moderate discomfort to the financial, as well as emotional, burdens connected with treatment. It is certainly questionable to rationalize high fees into an integral part of the therapy. But the doctor's own socio-economic guilt complexes and illusions need not impair his ability to charge appropriate fees.

Finally, understanding of the socio-economic setting and behavior, either rational or irrational, will help the practicing psychologist in appraising realistically his own social role and limitations. In the treatment of inner conflicts between and among drives and values, he will allow for the interaction between values and the socio-economic situation. He will thus beware of attempting to solve all the problems of his nation and the world by applied psychology or psycho-therapy. He will also recognize many of the personal problems of his patients as a mirror of socio-economic shortcomings which he needs to know about but cannot hope to cure in his professional role. Such shortcomings may have deep roots in, or interact with, the culture, history, socio-economic development stage, and world role of his nation.

In the light of this discussion, mental balance in society is not automatically assured by a high level of industrialization. Although this is not to be construed as an argument against modernization, it should be clear to the leadership of modernizing societies that this process will not in itself resolve the problems of happiness or mental adjustment, and may well create some new headaches. This sad fact, in turn, leads us to certain reflections on the general meaning of such concepts as modernization, development, and socio-economic system.

CHAPTER 7

Reflections on the Meaning of Development, Modernization, and Socio-Economic System

The recognition of the serious socio-psychological problems that survive, or originate, in an industrialized society has greatly contributed to a reappraisal in recent years of past, often uncritical, concepts of development, modernization, socio-economic system, and their interrelationship. Some decades from now, students of political psychology and economic semantics may write doctoral dissertations on the peculiar shift in the terminology and conception of "development" that occurred in the industrialized nations around the middle of the twentieth century. From the concept of "backward" countries that prevailed in the period of colonialism, they moved to "undeveloped" or "underdeveloped" nations. But some of these nations had had a highly sophisticated culture, in terms of artistic or religious life, centuries before the British Isles, not to mention North America, had been civilized or "developed." Accordingly the terminology changed later to the term "developing nations," but this really includes nearly everybody; or to the term "newly developing nations," but this does not fit entirely either as some as those referred to have actually been stagnating or regressing. The semantic preference thus switched to "modernization" or "transformation."

We should be misled once more if we interpreted these semantic fluctuations as a mere word game. The root of the uncertainty is in some second thoughts emerging both in the industrialized and in the modernizing countries on the meaning and purpose of the social processes concerned.

Some time ago Barbara Ward wrote an article in *The New York Times* under the title "We May Be Rich But They Are Happy." The perennial myth of the Happy Savage seems odd in countries which are plagued by near starvation, mass disease, slums, and illiteracy. Yet there is a modest nucleus of truth in it for some other countries which *are* underdeveloped in the Western sense yet have food, health, and schools approximately in the right quantities and distribution. They have, at the same time, kept themselves free from the crime waves, traffic jams, slum formation, air pollution, racial violence, and extreme inequalities that characterize some of the developed nations. Some years ago, when I served on a United Nations team advising the government of a very poor, very small, very new, but socially and culturally well-adjusted nation, I sometimes shuddered at the thought of what would happen if they carried out our recommendations! In the meantime, they have done so to some extent, although not in the order we recommended. From all one hears, they have no fewer problems now then they had then. This is by no means a unique experience in development policies. It should not, of course, be construed as an argument against all such policies or against technical assistance, but it supplies much food for thought.

Development, Growth, and Progress

In most of the Western academic discussions of related problems the concept of "economic growth" has been applied to quantitatively measurable increases in such data as production and income. Before the First World War, Schumpeter's famous "Theory of Economic Development" had also referred to certain historical processes in Western Europe and North America, but in the meantime the term "development" has come to refer chiefly to those areas which are regarded as not sufficiently developed yet in the present world. Even so, the implication has been basically the same: development has been seen mainly, if not exclusively, as a process in economics — the emergence of new economic institutions, such as industries and banking systems, extensive capital formation, rise in (and perhaps more equal distribution of) per capita incomes, and an increase in monetary stability.

All this remains valid as far as it goes, but within the last decade or two the concept of development has been enormously broadened. Bitter experience showed that the kind of development that remained confined strictly to the economic and financial level held little promise of being effective or durable. The development concept, therefore, has increasingly come to include the building of political institutions, either in the sense of a functioning public administration or in the sense of civil liberties and other guarantees of free expression, or both. Along with this come social concerns, such as population controls, public health, education for the masses, planned urbanization, welfare policies, community organization, and sometimes a drive for greater social equality or mobility.

However, even this expansion of the concept from the purely economic to the political and social levels has not satisfied a good many students and practitioners of development. The concept has come to include in addition a change or adjustment in many accustomed cultural patterns — for example, in the form and extent of family coherence, in the prevailing types of land tenure, (not only as a technical and economic arrangement but as a socio-cultural way of life as well), and beyond that, in the entire structure of the traditionally accepted and internalized values of most individuals in the culture concerned. This, in turn, has led to some rethinking of the impact of development upon personal satisfaction or, if you wish, happiness — a problem with which, of course, hundreds of philosophers ever since Plato, and countless millions of ordinary people have long been struggling. Is it the purpose of development, in the last resort, to make people happier, whatever this may mean? I could not begin to offer an answer here even if I had one, but this conceptual expansion of the development problem is remarkable.

Moreover, this expansion has an eminently practical impact. Some crucial decisions in nearly every country's policies depend on just these kinds of considerations, for the various types of emphases in modernization may be at odds with one another. To mention just one, the developed United States still faces many crucial decisions every year on whether or not to put, say, a six-lane highway through a scenic area, thus destroying its old character and the way of life of the residents. Which of the two possibilities represents progress, and which represents reaction?

In the modernizing countries, such choices are even more frequent. Almost invariably industrialization and the patterns of work that go with it destroy the traditional family coherence, and with it, the individual's sense of identity. Is the change worth its price, is the opportunity cost of modernization justified even in the economic sense, not to mention other values? Cost-benefit analysis in a purely economic context cannot provide the full answer. I am not, of course, arguing against modernization; I am just pointing out that disregard of its noneconomic effects may distort many important decisions about it, especially in the long-run. Moreover, we can no longer avoid the fact that one kind of development effect does not automatically follow from another, for instance, that higher per capita income — desirable as it may be — does not automatically lead to greater personal happiness, however defined; the only kind of progress which deserves this name.

Last but not least, such personal and cultural improvements may be at odds with that other side of economico-political change, a strengthening of military power, and with it, of the power role of the military groups within society. All too frequently this leads to a diversion of the new national identity, which has been enhanced by modernization, into a drive for national aggrandizement at the expense of less developed neighbors. This brings us to the broader problem of the function of the state in the process of modernization.

Development, Revolution, and the State

Many glib phrases have been used in the industrialized countries to describe the contemporary aspirations of modernizing nations and, especially, the new nations among them. "The revolution of rising expectations" is probably the best known of these phrases. The contrast to the formative concepts of Western industrialism a century or two ago is striking: before the Second World War, the predominant assumption in the West was that economic development was something that either happened spontaneously or not at all. This basic assumption characterized the otherwise widely divergent development theories of Adam Smith, Karl Marx, and Joseph Schumpeter. The revolution brought into the world by industrial capitalism was thought to be produced by competition and perhaps by the emergence of imaginative entrepreneurs. In the Marxian system of thought, it is true, both were going to run their course eventually, and capital export would no longer supply adequate outlets. The "ripe," stagnating capitalism was *then* (not before) going to be replaced by a classless society through the conscious action of the working class.

Today the conceptual and practical relationship between development and revolution is different. Rightly or wrongly, the modernizing nations (or, at least, their recent leadership groups) are not willing to wait either for stimuli provided by the industrialized countries or for the slow and somewhat uncertain effect of spontaneous development. The connotation of revolution in these areas is first, a fundamental (and, at the same time, rather fast) transformation of society, especially of the traditional power relations among social groups; and second, the use of public action aimed toward the modernization target with the help of changed power relations within the state if necessary. Development thus becomes a goal far exceeding higher per-capita income, GNP, or life expectancy, though all of these elements do remain in it. As pointed out in the second chapter, development is now increasingly meant to revolutionize the way of life, and all over Africa, as well as in other underdeveloped areas, a new kind of development socialism — sometimes of an ill-defined sort — has sprung up.

The active role of the state in the process of modernization is thus taken for granted in most areas, but actually the problem merely begins here. What *kind* of state is it that is to direct or foster modernization? Does either a democratic or an authoritarian regime per se encourage actual modernization? Should administrative efficiency be thought of as something that comes almost automatically with general modernization, or rather as a precondition of it? Is it promising or effective to issue an abstract development plan in the nature of a Declaration of Intention, even if no real machinery for its implementation has been set up? To ask this question is to negate it, yet a great many development plans and planners have not even perceived the difference. Is modernization possible without inflation, or shall we assume that the latter is inevitable in a development-minded state? In my experience, not many years ago in Brazil, for instance, even sophisticated businessmen and economists thought of inflation simply as one particular aspect of planned development, until they found out that they were getting severe inflation without development, either planned or unplanned. Since that time, an authoritarian military rule has attempted to reverse this trend.

It is the state, also, which is often expected to make such basic decisions as the emphasis upon industrial, rather than agricultural, development — as if the needs of almost any modernizing country did not require an agricultural basis for new industries along with their early utilization for greater agricultural productivity. Some-

140

times the state is also expected to exert pressure on the outside world so that it will grant continuous high prices for the exports of a monoculture country — say, coffee or copper — regardless of the world market situation and the extent of effective demand for such a commodity.

Such detailed controversies about the role of the state in modernization, while understandable, fail to throw much light upon the relationship between this process and the economic system. For decades the crucial dividing line among ideologies in the West was usually drawn between capitalism and socialism, or between free enterprise and collectivism. The decisive yardstick was the kind of ownership relations; it was based on either private or public property. It has been shown that outside the communist countries (in fact, even within some of them) this yardstick is no longer usable for a modernizing society, not to mention the fact that it is not very useful now for industrialized countries, such as the U.S. or France. In the modernization process today, the public and private sectors and action roles are usually intertwined. Israel offers a fine example of this new conceptual situation. More and more we are coming to think of the modernization process as such in terms of a new kind of economic system.

The most crucial distinction within this new conceptual framework is now that between totalitarianism and freedom as the socio-political basis of modernization. Even if we refrain (as we should) from interpreting freedom in the narrow sense of specific parliamentary and voting arrangements of this or that country in Western Europe or North America, the freedom to speak out, to dissent from the official policies, and to present to the people possible alternatives to the existing power structure will remain decisive. Nobody has yet presented a totalitarian system in a modernizing country (or in an industrialized nation, for that matter) that has been more efficient and honest, especially in the long-run, than are the admittedly slow procedures of many free societies.

The advantages of relative freedom as the basis of modernization, will be greatest when the population concerned enjoys a certain level of civic education, but this is precisely what a totalitarian regime cannot be expected to supply. In such a regime, there is no dividing line between education and propaganda. But even in a free society that is engaged in the process of modernization, crucial decisions must be taken on the *kind* of education that should be stressed, once a reasonably high level of literacy has been reached, or even before. Education for what? For making money as an individual more efficiently, or for being a community leader during the period of the great social and economic changes that modernization involves? Should education aim primarily at the acquisition of needed skills, at making people more effective as social beings, at making them happier as individuals, or something else? The point is that without widespread education, people will be unable to carry out modernization with freedom, but that abstract aims of education as such, perhaps an imitation of Western or Eastern ideas on curriculum and teaching methods, will not do. Education will be a fundamental part of modernization only if it is geared to the attitudinal changes required for this purpose, especially the individual and collective responsibility of the people themselves — not some inscrutable power above them or abroad — for their economic and social improvement.

Development versus Imitation

This brings up some more general questions about the meaning of development. If it involves basic changes in attitudes, either through the right kind of education or through other influences, what *kind* of attitudes (or perhaps we should add, *whose* attitudes in the outside world) can provide the model or goal for such changes? Can a Western-type "rationality" and will to action be consciously produced almost anywhere? To put it more bluntly, should modernizing nations think of themselves, or be thought of by others, as aiming at an imitation of the earlier development experience and industrial attitudes of the U.S., Russia, Japan, or any other industrialized nation of today?

We shall return later to the implications of this problem. Nowhere has it been treated more frequently, and perhaps more naively, than in the prolonged discussion on entrepreneurship as the supposed spearhead of modernization. We are using here the term entrepreneurship in the sense of innovation-minded initiative, not in the sense of running a business. Volumes have been written on how to arouse such a spirit in enough persons to shake a nation out of its sleepy traditionalist ways and, in particular, to generate a great upsurge of industrial development.

Now there *are* some individual examples of entrepreneurial spirit emerging in modernizing countries, such as Colombia and Pakistan, but even in this type of country any reliance on a repetition of the entrepreneurial experiences of Manchester, the *Ruhr-*

142

gebiet, or Detroit looks highly dubious. In my investigation of
business attitudes toward modernization in a large part of Latin
America, I found indications of an entrepreneurial spirit spearheading the great striving for modernization to be few and far
between.[1] Perhaps it has not been fair from the outset to assume
that certain European and North American experiences, with attitudinal change and with the development of new values regarding
national improvement through individual uncoordinated action,
could be repeated almost anywhere under a similar financial stimulus.

Once the difference in historical, cultural, and other conditions
is recognized, the search (quite popular only a few years ago) for
the best way to remove "obstacles" and to create the necessary
"prerequisites" for modernization becomes meaningless. What
looks to a foreign observer as an obstacle to change in a less
developed country may actually be a basic component of the cultural, historical, or economic background. And what to the West-
erner tends to be a prerequisite of modernization makes sense only
as long as he assumes that there is only one kind of condition
(namely, the kind his own country has experienced) under which
development can take off or reach a peak. The moment we recognize that there is more than one way to get socio-economic
changes under way and that there is more than one kind of modernization, this entire terminology loses its meaning.[2]

To restate the point, it is only if we equate modernization with
imitation of Europe or North America especially with such *quantitative* similarities as the trend of per capita income or investment
rates, that we shall expect such countries as Burma or Equador to
overcome the obstacles and lack of prerequisites for an imitation
of (Western-type) modernization. If, on the other hand, we do not
necessarily think of such processes in terms of remaking these
countries in the image of the U.S., France, or the Soviet Union,
then the development problem of the poorer countries must be
expressed in far broader although more realistic terms. It must be
defined in terms of exploring *their own* socio-economic potential,
both human and material, in line with their prevailing value system
and attitudes — not in order to preserve them unchanged but to be
realistic about the kind and pace of changes that are required in
that particular country, and about the concrete goals of modernization.

This does not mean, of course, that increased rates of per capita
income and investment are not of great importance, but it does

mean that the form, extent, and implementation of economic goals will vary widely. Moreover, none of the wealthier nations, no matter how modern and developed, should feel that it has the last word to offer on development or modernity. Greater humility and soul-searching on the part of these countries, without succumbing either to an exaggerated sense of guilt or to missionary delusions, are two of the implications of the approach just described.

Development and Independence

In fact, the entire relationship between the wealthier and the poorer nations is ripe for thorough rethinking on both sides. Those economists and statesmen in the industrialized countries who have been seeing the development aspirations of, say, Venezuela, Indonesia, or Nigeria merely in terms of improved productivity and standards of living have noticed only one side. The other, no less important side has been the quest for "real" independence which these nations — especially the new ones but including many that had existed for 150 years or so without having achieved a firm national identity — hope to build on a solid *economic* basis, far beyond the usual trappings of independence, such as a government palace, an army, postage stamps, and embassies.

But what *kind* of independence is it that these new or unsettled nations really want? Independence from what or whom? Does it perhaps express mere lack of concern, in one's own development plan, for the effects of this plan on others?

Obviously, there is mutual interdependence of all nations in this rapidly shrinking world; not even the most powerful can be independent in the absolute sense of the concept. Yet, nationalistic delusions of independence, even grandeur, along with a search for scapegoats abroad for one's own failures, have not been infrequent among some of the poorest, least stable nations. Ghana under Nkrumah or Indonesia under Sukarno are examples. Political independence from a specific (mostly Western but sometimes Eastern) government abroad is one thing; economic independence not only from world market fluctuations, but from other nations' development plans or aid is quite a different thing, especially when such an aim is associated with rapid industrialization.

If industrialization (perhaps in combination with a diversified agriculture) is intended to make a nation less vulnerable to the international fluctuations of demand and price for such products

144

as coffee, tin, or bananas, then the goal is certainly understandable. But this is a far cry from believing that the world owes a living to each of the poorer nations, and that the wealthy countries are under an economic, perhaps even a moral, obligation to buy at constantly high prices all the coffee or bananas which the poorer countries produce — regardless of whether these articles are wanted and whether the poorer countries concerned have given any active consideration to a possible diversification of their production and exports.

It is true that the principle of special favors to be given by the wealthier to the poorer nations has now been partly recognized by both sides, for example, in the deliberations of UNCTAD (United Nations Conference on Trade and Development). But this merely opens up a much broader question with which both sides will have to struggle during the years to come. What are the actual functions and limitations of international development aid, in contrast to the rather ambitious expectations of a few years ago, and is there any realistic possibility of a truly *international* policy in this field?

A few modest approaches to international cooperation for modernization seemed to be available in such experiments as the Central American Common Market before it bogged down; the five small countries included had expressed intentions to plan jointly their investment policies and industrial development. Generally, however, the world remained very far from an international policy, as the difficulties of the proposed UN Capital Development Fund showed. Perhaps this lag is unavoidable as long as there is basic ideological and political mistrust among the major world powers, not to mention the numerous other tensions in the world. But how much longer can both kinds of countries, the wealthier and the poorer, afford to rely on scattered, inadequate, and erratic development aid which is quite often at cross-purposes both in the various giving and in the various recipient nations (for example, when it is diverted for military purposes)?

A more promising approach which has been proposed by a World Bank study group, is to apply to the poorer nations mutually agreed upon criteria of economic performance to handicaps beyond their control that result from periodic market fluctuations for their chief products. This approach is to lead up to an internationally administered Supplementary Finance Scheme. But even on the more limited level of present-day aid policies, the modernizing nations can no longer avoid some basic decisions. In particular there is no such thing as foreign aid without some strings

145

attached, at least implicitly. The mere fact that aid is offered (or solicited) and accepted constitutes an inevitable modification of the independence of the recipient nation. The same, incidentally, is also true of foreign investment, although in a somewhat different way. The presence, perhaps dominance, of foreign capital (either public or private), foreign managers or technicians, foreign government advisers, or foreign financial experts constitutes almost by definition some degree of foreign interference in a nation's affairs, that is, a limitation to its independence. Both sides should be quite clear and honest about this.

The recipient nation, thus, cannot avoid a basic choice: is it willing to pay the price for faster modernization by accepting such limitations to its independence, or does it prefer to modernize more slowly without such limitations? Nobody can have his cake and eat it. To solicit and accept foreign aid and investment, and then to cry imperialism and to smash embassy windows when it actually comes is a practice which self-respecting nations should have outgrown. This, of course, does not excuse foreign governments, investors, or advisers for behaving like a bull in a china-shop, in shaky and vulnerable countries where most conditions are different from their own. [3]

Possibly, the underlying question is to what extent the general economic theories and beliefs from the West fit the conditions and needs of modernizing countries today. Merely to ask this question is very upsetting to many economists who have been brought up with the assumption that there are only two kinds of economics: good economics and bad economics, and that good economics applies in Calcutta, Conacry or La Paz no less than in Philadelphia or Düsseldorf. There is a certain nucleus of truth in this; but in the first place, the Western concepts of what is good economics have changed considerably from Adam Smith to Alfred Marshall, to Lord Keynes; and in the second place, can we really take it for granted that theories derived from the economic experiences of 18th, 19th, or 20th-century England (or any other Western country) are directly or even indirectly applicable to policy decisions in Djakarta or Brasilia today? I cannot begin to answer this complex question here, but we need to note, at least, that a good deal of soul-searching on this problem is now going on among economists in both the highly industrialized and the modernizing parts of the world. [4]

The Dilemmas of Modernization Policy

What new or modified policy principles in our period suggest themselves in the light of the preceding considerations? It would be absurd to claim that any of us presently have definitive answers to basic problems of modernization. Before we can speak of any clearcut solution, prolonged intellectual and perhaps political confrontations among the analysts and practitioners of modernization are required. But a few suggestions on the general direction in which such solutions should be sought are perhaps justifiable:

1. In the words of an outstanding development economist, the late Jorge Ahumada of Chile and Venezuela, "Economic development is not an economic problem." In fact, the whole concept of *economic* development as an isolated phenomenon of change may be wrong. What modernization policy really needs to be concerned with is the broad process of transformation of socio-economic institutions, administrative, legal, and political arrangements, and the underlying system of cultural values and attitudes. [5]

2. Modernization cannot be interpreted meaningfully as the remaking of an Asian, African, or South American culture and economic society in the image of the U.S., the U.S.S.R., Great Britain, or for that matter, of Japan or China. Although many industrial, agricultural, or managerial *techniques* from these countries can provide important guideposts for modernizing areas, socio-economic change in each of them, in a sense, must be of its own making and must be adjusted to its own background, needs and energies. In other words, there is not any one pattern or model of modernization which each modernizing nation must or can follow; beyond a certain technical point, it will inevitably be left to its own devices.

3. The role of foreign development aid, therefore, can only be strictly *complementary* to the national effort. In a way this is a commonplace statement, and yet there has been a great deal of intellectual and political confusion on the practical level. The modernizing nations should not assume that the wealthier ones *owe* them economic, social, or other improvements; and the wealthier powers should not become impatient if the recipients either hesitate or are unable to imitate successfully their experiences. If hundreds of millions of aid dollars seem to go down the drain without having produced the economic or political effects they were expected to, it can be simply because the modernizing countries themselves were not ready to make the attitudinal and

147

institutional adjustments needed, and even less ready to imitate the wealthy.

4. What from the perspective of advanced economies looks like modernization, development, or progress may sometimes conceal certain *destructive* effects of modern technology, industrialization, urbanization, and commercialization. I should like not to be misunderstood as preaching a *retour à la nature*. There is much room for *constructive* utilization of advanced techniques from abroad, but such favorable effects do not come automatically. Each modernizing nation (as well as its foreign advisers) needs to watch closely for a possible disruption of old values and ways of life, with demoralizing effects; in such cases, the population is left without a real chance to absorb the innovations through corresponding cultural adjustment.

5. Actually, the opportunity for the modernizing nations in our period goes far beyond such precautions. The newly transformed societies could potentially avoid some of the unhealthy aspects of the industrialization experience of others past and present, and could teach those others how to avoid exploitation, new inequalities, slum formation, educational lags, and racial troubles. In other words, these new societies have the possibility before them of building up something that is not only *not* a mere imitation of the wealthy, but that is actually *superior* to what the older patterns of development can offer, especially in terms of the basic values in life. Whether and where this will actually occur remains to be seen, but there is every reason for the industrialized nations to consider the transformation of other areas today as a unique opportunity to search their own souls and to re-examine the meaning of their economic and social achievements and failures.

Modernization and Socio-Economic System

Every year that goes by increasingly emphasizes the fact that the time-honored Western concepts of capitalism, socialism, communism, and fascism as the main types of socio-economic systems do not fit very well the process of change in modernizing areas, nor are they really descriptive of it. The more we discover about the nature of modernization and about what exactly happens in its course — and we still have quite a way to go before we fully grasp these happenings — the clearer it becomes that modernization can be meaningfully understood only as a continuing process over a

148

long period, not as the establishment of a more or less stabilized system whose legal, operational, and attitudinal principles are well-defined, even though details may keep changing. In one sense, modernization is precisely a striving for definition of the *aims* of the drive for change, not only for the achievement of specific, well-defined institutions. As we have pointed out, what used to be called development actually represents a broad process of socio-cultural transformation of which economics offers only one aspect, although certainly an important one. By the same token, changes in property relations, which have traditionally been seen as the chief indicator of change over from one economic system to another, are of very limited relevance for this socio-cultural transformation.

From another angle, development processes in the sense of broad transformation almost invariably show in each country certain elements derived from *several* socio-economic systems, in varying proportions, along with some elements that are characteristic only of the area or culture in question. These processes represent a constant variation both of a convergence and divergence (and sometimes a seemingly crazy mixture) of more conventional socio-economic systems.[6] Some specific aspects of these relationships will be discussed later. First, however, it must be pointed out that — despite frequent semantic overlapping or confusion — competing development ideologies, regardless of their political slant or specific emphasis, actually all have a different focus from capitalist, socialist, and other Western-type ideologies even when the same words are used. Development in itself is the *focus* of national or group ideology in every modernizing area, and the older Western concepts mentioned merely provide the trappings, if not the window dressing, for a basic aspiration for socio-cultural transformation.

An unemotional discussion of the relationship of socio-economic systems to the contemporary processes of modernization can bring much needed clarity regarding the uses and limitations of the system concept, both in the past and in the contemporary world. The first requirement along these lines is some further clarification of three basic concepts: development, modernization, and socio-economic system.

The Development Problem Restated

The meaning of economic development in relation to broad

149

socio-cultural transformation has been discussed earlier. The gist of the problem is a clear-cut distinction between mere economic growth on the basis of existing institutional arrangements; a basic change in economic structure and in the relations between social groups; technological and organizational modernization; and a far reaching transformation of society including all of these elements and, in addition, a gradual change in values and attitudes.

Beyond this question, however, lies another of even greater import. Do we want to view development or modernization essentially as a process of catching up with the wealthier nations, or largely as a *qualitatively* different process of change in each nation and society concerned? [7]

Both the less developed nations and their wealthier mentors have found out through painful experience that chasing a single cause of economic underdevelopment offers little promise. One cannot achieve an increase in per capita income or in the level of productivity without crucially affecting the type of land tenure, financial habits, social power structure, public administration, and the broad perception among people of what does or does not matter in life. As for the emulation of Western institutions, it has indeed been shown to be possible, within limits, in such matters as technology, literacy programs, and marketing techniques. But it has also been found to be subject to far-reaching variations from one area to another, with regard to such factors as consumer preferences, saving habits, institutionalized corruption, entrepreneurship, religious norms, pecuniary incentives, attitudes toward work and leisure, and a myriad of other basic influences.

It is not very promising, therefore, to interpret the processes of change in the modernizing areas today as an incipient or required adaptation to the economic, social, and cultural ways of life that were developed elsewhere. *Some* learning from the past experiences of the developed nations is certainly possible and necessary, but any expectation that the pattern everywhere will sooner or later be American-type capitalism or Russian-type communism would be unrealistic.

The Meaning of Modernization

The danger just discussed also applies potentially to the concept of modernization. "Modern" can be interpreted as meaning whatever is practiced in the United States, Great Britain, Holland, and the Soviet Union insofar as technology and, to some extent, con-

150

sumption patterns are concerned. For several reasons this is not the meaning, however, in which the concept of modernization has been used in this discussion.

First, everything is not modern in the countries just mentioned. Housing shortages, corruption, violence, racial troubles, air and water pollution, bureaucratic inefficiency, transportation bottlenecks, waste, oppression and exploitation of minority groups, hatreds and irrational actions in private and public life — all these exist on a sizeable scale in the modern societies and therefore, they simply cannot serve as a model for modernizing countries.

Second, changes in technology and consumption patterns, while important, do not exhaust the amount and quality of social change that characterize a meaningful concept of modernization. In fact, neither technology nor consumption can change in a far-reaching and lasting way unless the social structure, the institutional framework, the organization of production, the prevailing traditions and attitudes of the people (especially the reference groups) are also transformed. All of this will rarely occur simultaneously, or in the same degree, but it is the *combination* of all these changes over a period of time that adds up to modernization in the sense in which we have been using this concept.

Third, modernization is usually associated with bringing a nation's functioning "up to date" in the sense, not of reaching the level of some model country, but of bringing that functioning in line with that nation's own felt needs and aspirations — which, of course, *are* frequently influenced to some extent by the example of its neighbors or other countries. Population pressure or world market prices for basic commodities will likewise influence the felt needs and aspirations of a given nation, through their objective effect on its condition. But this also means that there is (and must be) more than one kind of modernization. Instead of everybody blindly imitating a foreign model of modern society, each nation modernizes in its own way, although the various national patterns of transforming the institutions and attitudes from the past will overlap or resemble one another in many cases. Modernization, in summary, will not represent one set of transforming or imitating measures to be applied everywhere indiscriminately, but a general principle with a variety of possible policies for its implementation.

These considerations also apply to the resulting kinds of economic system. If modernization is to be interpreted in the sense just discussed, one will not expect that capitalism, communism or any other specific ism from Western or Eastern Europe, or North

America, will be adopted by all the modernizing nations of Latin America, Asia, and Africa.

The Meaning of Economic System

In the past, the concept of "economic system" referred mainly to property arrangements, especially regarding the means of production, although such factors as the respective degrees of market freedom and central planning, and the political groups and forces in charge of administering these arrangements were usually also included in some manner. The distinction between the *Idealtypus* of each (static) system, its abstract or theoretical formulation, however defined, and the actual (dynamic) institutional arrangements in historical reality was not always made clear; nor was the impact of attitudinal, not merely institutional, differences between the various systems (for example, in their appeal to various kinds of motives and incentives for desired economic action) clarified. "Prototypes" of economic systems, distilled from historical experiences, were closer to reality without being completely explanatory. [8]

How useful, then, are general models of economic systems in the contemporary world, and do they help us in understanding the widespread drive for modernization? Shall we keep classifying countries with a substantial share of private ownership as capitalist even if some key industries are state owned, as in Great Britain, France, Austria, Mexico, and India? Shall we keep classifying as capitalist a country with mainly private title to industrial and commercial property as in the United States, even though this legal title is limited by a thousand regulations, by public budgets of hundreds of billions of dollars, and by a fiscal and monetary policy that steers private enterprises in specific ways? What is to be classified as a socialist system? Sweden, Great Britain, Egypt, India, and Chile all claim some degree of socialism in targets and institutions, while the communist regimes in the U.S.S.R., Yugoslavia, Cuba, and China, though profoundly different from one another, all persist in using the term socialism to describe their own present condition.

Even more fundamental, what can be a meaningful *yardstick* of economic system, since the old distinction between types of essentially legal property arrangements does not seem to be very helpful any longer? One possible yardstick would be the process of pric-

152

ing; a related one, the prevailing kind of market mechanism; a third, the centralized or decentralized allocation of resources; a fourth, the legal system of ownership, especially of the means of production; a fifth, the ("meta-economic") social values and aims underlying economic arrangements and decisions no matter which allocation or pricing technique is used.[9] Personally, I consider the fifth yardstick to be the most meaningful and promising. The distinction between economic principles based on military or political conquest of other nations, and those based on speedy industrialization, on getting rich quick, or on good education for the rank and file, for example, would seem to be far more important than the distinction between public and private titles to certain types of property.

Capitalism, Socialism, and Communism Today

In the industrialized countries, the various economic systems have been gradually but unmistakably losing their original meanings, or at least their unambiguous meanings, to the extent that such systems ever had them. We have mentioned already the perennial discrepancy and confusion between abstract socio-economic isms in a theoretically pure sense and the various institutional arrangements whose spokesmen have chosen to use the theoretical terms without in practice approaching their abstract meaning, with the exception of some very brief historical periods.

What has contemporary capitalism in the United States in common with the economic system that Marx and Engels were writing about in the 1840s, or even in the 1880s? It has only the legal form of private ownership titles for many (by no means all) means of production. Actually, even this legal form is quite different for the decisive segment of the economy where ownership is private but not individual. In the most developed countries, the corporate collectivism that has taken over is about as different from the old owner-manager capitalism, as it is from a state-owned corporate structure; and the geographic range of corporate collectivism has gradually been spreading.

If we look at the programmatic statements of Western socialist parties after the Second World War, we find that even in the West the term socialism no longer describes a reasonably well-defined economic system.[10] The old definition of socialism as public ownership of all the means of production has evaporated. Western socialists still support (as do various nonsocialists) the state ownership of specific industries or plants which are considered vital to the economy, monopolistic, or representing an unusual power concentration. However, welfare policies in health, education, and housing, along with more or less Keynesian application of fiscal and monetary measures for continuous full employment, have come to the fore and are shared with many brands of progressivism and reform-mindedness in general.

The communist monolith of Lenin's and Stalin's days likewise has been changing fundamentally, with many zigzags and setbacks. Not only has the political unity been broken in recent years by the showdown between China and Russia, and much earlier by the defection of Yugoslavia; but the economic principles of communism have come to be interpreted in communist countries in widely varying and changing ways. Central pricing and marketing have given way in various places to substantial leeway for individual plant management; competition for manpower, even for customers, among the state-owned plants has been on the increase; workers' control of each plant is far-reaching in at least one country, and peasant ownership of a large proportion of the land applies in various ways to several countries.[11] Which of these institutional arrangements, past or present, ranging from Yugoslavia to Russia and from Cuba to China, represents the true economic system of communism? All or none.

Finally, there is the forgotten man of economic systems, at least insofar as some of the Western nations are concerned: fascism. A whole generation of Western Europeans, not to mention Americans, has grown up to whom the concept of fascism is altogether alien. Mussolini's corporate state and Hitler's regimented economy, in both cases permanently oriented toward aggressive war, have receded into history. But the post-Salazar Portugal and Franco Spain are still there, and fascist movements and mentalities remain fairly widespread in the world. The basic difficulty taxonomically-oriented economists have had with defining a fascist economic system has always been that it has never lent itself very well to classification. There are two reasons for this: first, because its economic institutions and policies have always served primarily noneconomic goals, such as (in large countries) preparation for a coming war and conquest; and, second, because the very nationalism in its extreme form that has characterized each fascist movement or regime has brought an intentional, if not always successful, search for distinctive ideologies and policies in each national fascist party.

154

Each of the old economic systems has thus undergone conceptual disintegration during the historical process. At the same time, they have all developed certain distinctive aspects not only in the technology, but in the managerial organization of their economy.

Entrepreneurship, Management, and Development

In Schumpeter's concept of entrepreneurship as the driving force of economic development, the entrepreneur was clearly associated with the capitalist system. Only there was the innovating mentality and action thought to be possible. In fact, it was thought that the system had actually been brought into being by the emergence of this kind of person (although Schumpeter in his later years was by no means optimistic about the future of this system). [12]

In the modernizing economies of our period, the connection is by no means seen to be so clear-cut. In the first place, there are many remaining questions on the actual role of individual entrepreneurs in the process of economic development, on the factors that generate such individual personalities and make them effective, and on the part that "unbalanced growth," in Hirschman's sense, leaves to the individual entrepreneur. [13] In addition, there are now numerous examples of the "use and stimulation" of private entrepreneurship by public development planners. Important instances also exist of governments now taking over — in a modified way, to be sure — much of the entrepreneurial function which Schumpeter associated so clearly with private enterprise. In the modernizing countries of Latin America, the Nacional Financiera in Mexico, the Cauca Valley Corporation in Colombia, the CORFO in Chile, and various comparable institutions in Puerto Rico and other countries are examples.

Possibly even more important today, there is the impact of *collective* entrepreneurship, along with executive teamwork in a broader sense, in the large private corporations in industrialized and, to a lesser degree, in modernizing countries. Teams of professionally trained executives are gradually taking over both the day-to-day decisions on all levels and the entrepreneurial decisions at the top. And the difference between executive functions in a privately owned and in a publicly owned enterprise is shrinking. Other variables have become more important than this one; among these are the degree and kind of the executive's education and training, the absence or presence of family links and nepotism, the

155

personal ability or inability to work in a group and to get along with people, the respective degrees of conformity and initiative, innovative imagination, and so forth. The legal, political, and cultural setting certainly remains of considerable importance, but the degree to which professional executives have become interchangeable between privately and publicly owned enterprises, and in a broader sense, between formerly unbridgeable economic systems, has grown historically to an unforeseen extent.

Western Reform Movements and Modernization

How have the older movements of social protest and reform in industrialized countries, especially labor and socialist movements, responded to the challenge of underdevelopment in Asia, Latin America, and Africa, and to the recent aspirations of these areas for modernization and greater prosperity? This question has been discussed in chapter 2, and we need here only to relate it more closely to the theme of the present chapter.

Until the Second World War, social reform groups and parties in Europe and North America paid little attention to the less developed areas. To the limited extent that they were discussed at all, their socio-economic problems were seen merely as one aspect of Western colonialism. The attention of these social reform movements was focused on exploitation and oppression in their own respective countries. Such international cooperation as there was, especially in the Labor and Socialist International, was centered unsuccessfully on the prevention of war and, between the two world wars, on warding off the onslaught of communism and fascism.

Moreover, even their domestic action concentrated essentially on reforming the existing economic system, partly by building into it some elements of social welfare and labor organization and legislation, and partly — in an historically diminishing degree — by aiming at the nationalization of the means of production. It took the Western-type reform movements, of both the Marxist and Fabian variety, quite some time to understand that the populations of poverty-stricken countries (or their avant-garde) were not prepared to await transformation until they were industrially "ripe," and that their main problem or aspiration was not the nationalization of existing (in fact, mostly non-existing) industries but the rapid and extensive creation of *new* ones, along with other forms of broad social transformation. Moreover, these peoples fre-

156

quently found the specific ownership arrangement of their long-range preference to be at odds with their most urgent needs for socio-economic change.

The modernizing areas, therefore, had little use for imported concepts of economic system, even though they used the same terminology extensively. In particular, they liked to classify themselves as socialist-oriented, sometimes as Marxist, and the countries of Western Europe and North America as capitalist in the sense of the 1840s. Actually, the change in economic system which reform movements in Western Europe and North America had in mind was almost meaningless for nations that first had to *generate* a modern industrial and social structure, before being able to *change* it on the lines of either the Fabians or the Marxists. Conversely, the concepts of economic system which Western movements had been using as the backbone of their own struggle for social change turned out to be of far less general validity than they had long assumed. It was this lack of communication between the Western movements for change in the existing economic system, and the non-Western movements for modernization, which enhanced in the latter, in their impatience for quick remedies, the propensity to adopt totalitarian solutions or pseudo-solutions. [14]

Development Planning and the Economic System

Somewhat similar considerations apply to the relationship between planning and the economic system. As mentioned earlier, some decades back, Western socialists, especially those influenced by Marxism, used to interpret the coming change in economic systems as a transition to public ownership of all the means of production. This transition, in turn, was reasoned to be the only possible base for broad economic planning which would eliminate the old chaos of capitalist market competition with its cyclical, and historically worsening, waves of unemployment. Planning was thus interpreted as possible only on the basis of public ownership and as encompassing the whole range of existing production facilities.

Since then the concept of planning has undergone essential changes in Western reform movements. It now refers to a coordinated economic policy — usually emphasizing economic growth — including private and public enterprise, foreign trade, monetary and fiscal measures for economic stability, and every other important aspect of economic activity regardless of the kinds of owner-

157

ship title concerned. Even so, this revised concept of planning in the industrialized countries of the West is of very limited help in meeting the needs of modernizing areas.

In modernizing countries, planning refers essentially to the intended creation of *new* productive facilities in a coordinated manner. This planning includes sufficient stimuli to private modernizing activities, an infrastructure including a reliable administrative apparatus, and the incorporation or establishment of some public enterprises. These are the elements of a grand design for structural transformation of the economy and society. Such a design is not always translated into action with full success and is sometimes even construed as a substitute for economic policy.[15] The difference, in other words, is that the purpose of planning is not a mere rearrangement of existing economic facilities in the interest of a higher growth rate, but the intended creation of new ones along with social improvements. Thus far, the prevailing approach to development planning has been "teleological," rather than "genetic," and has rarely been undertaken within a framework of regional cooperation.

The planning process in a modernizing economy, even more than in an industrialized one, is inevitably tied to the determination of the values that are to guide it. Is it to be the purpose of development planning to try to emulate this or that wealthier country? There is no such thing as abstract planning for development or modernization in general; the question "planning for what" cannot be avoided. For example, the relative weight to be given to the incorporation of remote rural groups (say, the Indians of the South American *altiplano*) into the national economy and society, as against a priority for quick industrialization of a limited area or the possible choice between an emphasis on mass education and a preference for fiscal stabilization, show the necessity of a specific value orientation in development planning. Another such decision concerns the extent and forms of allowing for the *social costs* (as well as some social benefits) in economic changes when designing and implementing a development plan.[16]

The experience of modernizing economies within the communist orbit can only be mentioned here, and this includes the transformation of the Soviet economy during the last forty years. In these cases, the nationalization of the limited industrial facilities in existence (and, in some but not all of these countries, of the land) has been accompanied by the planned establishment of a new industrial structure on a large scale. Without going into the details of this process and of the recent changes in the degree of

158

managerial centralization in the pricing and marketing system, and other aspects of their now more industrialized economies, it is clear that this whole experience has not followed the nineteenth century assumption that a ripe capitalist system would be followed by an equally developed but collectively organized classless society. Doubtless, the future historian will see the historic achievement of Russia not in the change from one system of ownership to another, but in the industrialization and agrarian modernization of the country (largely on the basis of newly created productive facilities) within a few decades.

Is Economic System Still A Valid Concept?

Since the old concepts of economic system, based on Western experience, have lost much of their validity there and seem even less applicable to the modernizing economies, and since these economies — even including to some extent those under communist control — employ a variety of methods of ownership, allocation, and stimulation of *new* economic activities, how useful is the concept of economic system as such?

Here again, when the discussion is confined to the *Idealtypus* of this or that abstract economic (or socio-economic) system, with conscious and explicit avoidance of applications to existing economic arrangements, some didactic usefulness of the concept remains. On the other hand, when a typology of economic systems in the conventional sense is applied to the actual scene today, not only semantic, but intellectual confusion is bound to result from an uncritical application to modernizing areas and their transformation processes of such traditional concepts as capitalism or socialism, even in their prototype forms.

It seems to be far more promising, therefore, to replace this outmoded conceptual framework by a sliding scale of *many* changing combinations — not necessarily convergences — of socio-economic policy aims and methods, old and new, including ownership arrangements, pricing and allocation, and stimuli to both the private and public economic activities. In the case of modernizing economies, this combination, with its variations according to country and industrial stage, can best be expressed in terms of general and sectoral targets and in terms of the specific methods of development planning, policies and stimuli for modernization that are actually used under the conditions of each area (especially in regard to the structural changes and transformation effects that have occurred or are under way). Such a fluid approach to the endless variety of processes and policies of modernization appears much more meaningful than a reliance on a more or less static set of institutional arrangements squeezed into the conceptual strait-jacket of past experiences from Europe and North America.

Should the modernization process itself be seen as a socio-economic system, among other things? In the light of the preceding discussion, the answer to this question is a qualified yes, with special application to currently modernizing areas. The process of modernization cuts across feudalism, capitalism, socialism, communism, fascism, and perhaps some other socio-economic systems in the conventional sense. Interpreted as broad socio-cultural transformation, the *essence* of the process, though not the sequence or combination of steps, is largely the same no matter what ideological or terminological framework is used. The real reservation to be made here concerns the fact that while the process of modernization represents an economic system among other things, it is far more than this: it is a socio-cultural system within which economics represents a "subsystem." The changes in production methods and productivity, technology and organization, ownership arrangements, and allocation criteria are but one aspect of the broad transformation referred to earlier. Modernization thus *absorbs* and *modifies* the older concept of a change over of socio-economic systems and adds to it a number of noneconomic factors such as change in cultural attitudes, administrative procedures, and power relations among social groups.

This last aspect is of special importance. While the nature of the modernization process may not differ fundamentally regardless of the mixture of institutional methods used, the social and political forces behind such measures do vary a great deal, and in one sense the distinction according to *who* may be more important than according to *what*. In other words, different social power groups may carry out technically similar processes of modernization with different efficiency and motivation. The results will vary not so much according to how much private ownership is used, for example, but according to which group — the big landowners, the peasants, the new industrial workers, the emerging professional or middle classes, or any other group — will implement modernization and how these will carry out innovations in the social and economic institutions, political and administrative procedures, and cultural attitudes.

160

CHAPTER 8

The Crisis of the Development Idea

This final chapter is a summary and conclusion based on the preceding discussions. Even at the risk of some unavoidable repetition, it may be helpful to sum up the trend of thought and analytic findings offered in this book.

Despite some available examples of successful development, usually in a technological sense but at times involving increased rates of economic growth or per capita income, the international development idea is in a state of fundamental crisis whose full extent is but slowly emerging from the subsiding waves of yesterday's enthusiasm. The crisis is not confined to financial and political frustrations, which are frequent and lead to an ugly mood. It encompasses the very root of the development idea. This has been brought out by various reactions to the dubious results of the first United Nations Development Decade.

The crisis expresses itself in a variety of ways. One of its most evident aspects consists of the disappointment of the aid-giving countries with the results achieved. This is matched by the dismay of recipient countries with the aid received, if not with the whole course of development. In particular, yesterday's interpretation of modernization as imitation of the developed nations has given way to the discovery of the painful headaches of the donors themselves. Moreover, the belief in technology as the answer to development needs is now confronted with the effects of technological change on natural resources, employment, and peace.

The question is raised frequently whether development should not be seen in terms of a far-reaching social revolution, and whether consequently the industrialized nations of the West, despite all the development aid they offer, do not essentially constitute an obstacle to this social necessity. This situation is interpreted by many as indicating a need for some kind of socialism, which some of them see in terms not only of planned development, but of a totalitarian drive for new institutions and motivations. Others criticize, along somewhat related lines, the entire concept of economic development and prefer to replace it by the broader concept of socio-cultural transformation involving basic changes in values and attitudes, although not excluding economic growth. There are even a few examples of virtual refusal to develop. More questions are raised on both sides — the developing and the developed — regarding the extent to which development, however interpreted, can be aided from the outside. These various aspects of the overall crisis of the development idea will now be discussed in greater detail.

The Disappointment of the Aid-Giving Countries

In the fifties and well into the sixties, enthusiasm was great in the industrialized nations, most of all in the United States, for aiding the underdeveloped countries (as they were then called) in getting out of their abysmal poverty and beginning to enjoy the fruits of civilization. This latter-day version of "The White Man's Burden" had several variations. One of them was simply the fear of communism or revolution in poverty-ridden countries unless they were helped effectively to overcome their plight. A cruder, but perhaps more candid, approach was represented by the belief that every problem or danger in the world could be resolved by spending enough money, in this case three or four billion dollars a year on the part of the United States and comparable amounts on the part of other Western nations. Spending one percent of a nation's income for development aid came to be considered a fairly generous or, at least, a sufficient contribution toward the solution of the world's development tasks.

A related but somewhat different interpretation of development aid consisted of a new brand of power politics. You would offer a poor nation money, technicians, and weapons, and it would become (and presumably remain) your friend, perhaps your ally. Consequently, aid was focused in some cases, such as French support to West Africa, on former colonies of the Western power concerned; aid was little more than an extension of the former

162

colonial policy. Whether this kind of aid was really promising, or for how long, is another question. The Soviet Union and other nations of Eastern Europe, in a limited degree Communist China as well, applied very similar methods to their own protégés, especially in Africa and the Middle East, likewise with uncertain results in a longer run.

It would be unjustified, though, to overlook the humanitarian motivation which was part of the public attitude, if rarely of government policy, in the movement for development aid in the rich countries. The old impulse toward generosity or else toward old-fashioned "do-gooding" in the United States, Great Britain and some other countries of the West had a definite, if not always realistically conceived, share in the urge to aid the poor.

All these approaches to development aid, different as they were, involved the expectation of some kind and degree of gratitude on the part of the recipient nations. This applied most obviously to the humanitarian approach, but it included the money cure, the weapons cure, and even straight power politics. In each case, it was expected that the recipient nation would build up some kind of moral and political dependence on the aid-giving nation. In a few cases such expectations were actually fulfilled in the short run, at least; but these examples were far exceeded by those in which the result of aid came to be not gratitude but resentment, hatred or contempt. The psychological mechanism involved was not so very different from frequent individual reactions to help supplied: the recipient will never forgive the donor for having made him feel inferior or dependant on other people's aid — and for having *expected* gratitude. Shame feelings for having asked for or accepted aid turn sooner or later into hostility. The moral for aid-givers is that aid should never be given on the implicit assumption of a trade, be it in terms of political support or of moral gratitude. When the aid is not offered more or less unconditionally, save for strictly technical requirements of effective use, the giver is almost inevitably in for disappointments.

The Dismay of the Developing Nations

Insofar as generalizations are possible, the thinking of the developing nations follows different lines, but disappointment is no less widespread. The somersaults of the terminology used since the late forties have merely reflected the conceptual and psychological

163

vagaries of the thing itself. Gone are the days when the rich used to speak of "backward" nations or populations in Asia, Africa or Latin America; some of whom, while poor, had experienced a rich cultural life — and a continuous if sometimes very slow economic development — at a time when North America and Western Europe were populated by a few savages. The term "undeveloped", often used in conjunction with "underdeveloped," did not fare much better after a while and aroused resentments. The United Nations and other organizations and governments then adopted the term "developing nations" which is more polite but again misses the point. After all, the developed nations also keep developing, but this is not the only shortcoming of the term.

In the first place, many of the nations concerned are not developing at all; they are stagnating or going backward insofar as their economic growth rates, per capita income, socio-economic institutions, life expectancy, degree of industrialization, educational and political levels, and other conventional criteria are concerned. Or they are developing at much too slow a pace to cope with their rate of population increase and with the aspirations of their leading groups or else of the poverty-stricken, long dormant but now awakening masses, which have found out that even an impressive rate of economic growth or industrialization does not automatically relieve the twin scourges of unemployment and underemployment. In any case, these nations have become impatient, resentful or frightened. Their leadership tends to shake off the responsibility for social evils. What is more natural in such a situation than a search for villains, preferably foreign ones? This absolves both the rulers and the masses from responsibility for the evils in existence and helps to rationalize their own inertia. This explanation, however, does not imply that the foreign influences are not at fault at all.

Actually, the roots of the growing dismay of the developing nations go much deeper than this. The halo of the developed nations has faded and has in fact begun to look quite shabby. Inflation, balance-of-payments problems, inequality of incomes and wealth, unemployment, armaments, terror actions at home and abroad, crime, drug addiction, air and water pollution, urban blight, race troubles, youth rebellion, transportation chaos and many other headaches of the developed nations make many observers on both sides wonder what the much-advertised development is all about. In the words of the British expert Dudley Seers, "After all, in what sense is South Africa more developed than

Ghana, or Kuwait than the U.A.R., or the United States than Sweden?" [1].

Development as Imitation?

Twenty years ago the essence of development appeared to be quite clear to people in the developed and the developing countries alike. It seemed to consist of a process of catching up, on the assumption that mankind was, or should be, developing in a single direction. Implicitly, the wealthy kept saying to the poor: "See how rich, efficient, diligent, smart and happy we are? All you need to do is to follow the path we are showing you." Obstacles to development needed to be removed and prerequisites were to be established. The poor tended to accept this approach, to the limited extent that they were able to perceive an alternative to their age-old way of life or even to see it in terms of poverty.

Some residual attitudes of this kind still persist on both sides, but on the whole the atmosphere has been changing rapidly. The irrelevance of a sizable proportion of Western (and, for that matter, Eastern) economic theory for the modernization needs of large parts of the world has become conspicuous. Moreover, the headaches of the wealthier nations now include the rebellion of the young in their own ranks against the felt emptiness of ruling theories in general and the developed way of life with its failure to form meaningful values; a rebellion which, to be sure, has thus far been mostly of a negative character but has not escaped the attention of the modernizing nations.

The imitative approach, therefore, is rapidly reaching its historical limits. It is now being displaced by the other extreme: resentment toward the successful, usually while still asking for and receiving their money but accompanied by increasing contempt. Basically, the resentment stems partly from the belief that their successes, at least in the economic sense, have been due to exploitation of the poor at home and abroad, and partly from the discovery that the rich have been unable to solve their own basic problems, and that in fact, the very creation of wealth has created some new ones. The rich nations thus appear plagued by problems beyond their control. In extreme cases, they become an object of pity while still being envied for their material wealth. In this highly contradictory way, the imitation urge has been yielding to resentment.

165

A case in point is presented, in a very special way, by the attitude of many nonaligned (actually underdeveloped) nations toward Israel. An observer from Mars might assume that these nations would consider Israel an admirable model of what a new, small desert nation surrounded by enemies could achieve in a few years, mainly through its own effort; and that they would in addition be impressed by the strong socialist labor movement and the government which had emerged from it and had established a large public sector in the developing economy.

Actually, the attitudes which arose toward Israel in the developing nations (by no means the Arab countries only) during the sixties have been entirely different. These attitudes have variously been interpreted in terms of a hatred of the lazy toward the diligent or of the ineffective toward the successful, of a rebellion of inertia against relentless self-help, or of those who feel guilty for developing slowly or not at all against those who by their own successes *make* them feel guilty. In addition, the Israelis have often been associated with "white" while the Arabs, paradoxically, have not. Others see the reason for the resentment in the fact that the leading Israeli groups have thus far usually been of a European background and that Israel has been supported from American sources. As a result, it is associated with Western imperialism, which somehow is seen as more vicious than the Eastern brand. Finally the Egyptians, Syrians, Iraquis, Algerians and Libyans have managed to associate the Arab cause with revolution or socialism even though these countries, not to mention Saudi Arabia or Morocco, continue to show glaring examples of ancient or mediaeval types of exploitation and oppression.

The Israeli development aid to West and East African countries in particular but also to Asia and Latin America, ranging from agriculture and irrigation to youth organization, health and medicine, and vocational training, made many friends in the short run and many enemies in the long run. Aside from the possible reasons listed earlier, nations like individuals often cannot forgive others for having helped them, especially if the aid-giver himself has demonstrated what can be achieved through self-help. There is one aspect of development where for the time being aid is still being widely solicited from the richer: technology. It is here where the imitative approach remains fairly influential, even though reservations have been on the increase.

Development and Technology

Until very recently, imitative development was seen largely in terms of a technological modernization in conjunction with extensive industrialization and a corresponding rise in per capita product and income. Some of this interpretation has survived but many qualifications have been added in recent years. One of them refers to the *kind* of technology that is best suited to the situation of a small market populated by peasants or new workers with little industrial experience, low incomes, and very limited consumer aspirations. Questions have been raised especially on the rationale of using the latest techniques, usually based on costly imported capital equipment. This presupposes, first, a large market which may require working common-market agreements among several countries; second, a sufficient supply of hard currencies; and third, extensive training facilities which can keep pace with the supply of equipment.

Even so, serious questions remain regarding the effect of industrial modernization on the employment situation. Only yesterday it was widely assumed that the new industries and the resulting economic growth in general would absorb the widespread unemployment, including the rural underemployment, that characterizes most underdeveloped economies. We know now that industrialization does not necessarily have this effect, especially if it is based on capital-intensive technology. In most of the countries which have undergone some degree of industrialization during recent decades, unemployment and underemployment remain a severe problem. In a good many of them, it has even grown worse — not because of industrialization but, at least, despite it. Awareness of social effects, such as changes in family coherence, has also increased.

At the same time, technological modernization has invariably raised the military potential of these nations; this is also being stimulated more directly by the great powers and some smaller ones for straight political power reasons. The result is that not a few of the same nations which for alleged lack of resources cannot manage to solve their unemployment problem, to clear out their slums, or to wipe out illiteracy, somehow do find the means to threaten or actually fight with their equally poverty-stricken neighbors. Pakistan, Bangladesh and India offer one example, Egypt or Syria another, El Salvador and Honduras a third, Uganda and Tanzania a fourth; several others could be added. It would, of course, be unjustified to blame technological progress alone for aggressive urges among nations, but this progress makes them more destructive and effective militarily at the expense of genuine development of an economic and social nature.

Even where technological modernization is channelled into peaceful pursuits, more advanced technology does not automatically bring equally higher productivity. Frequently, the new industrial worker takes longer to develop new attitudes toward work than to build up aptitudes. The required regularity of his presence in the plant, performance of the job, teamwork, and the association of higher productivity with greater income usually take much time to become firmly anchored in the mind of the new worker. Similarly, the new industrial manager rarely shakes off right away the authoritarian mentality of the upper classes from which he came, and even more slowly converts himself into an innovating entrepreneur. Managers and, to a lesser extent, specialized workers may undergo training abroad in the technical aspects of their occupations, but they typically face serious problems of readjustment at home in terms of attitudes and social roles. This is not an argument against the application of modern technology to newly developing countries, but it shows that technology itself is not a panacea in the process of development. Apparently more fundamental changes are required in order to make this process meaningful.

Development and Revolution

The conviction that not only technological but social changes of a fundamental nature are required to bring about real development is now rather widespread, though by no means universal, in Latin America, Africa and Asia. Marxist ideologies or, at least, terminologies are widely used to explain or justify the revolution required. It is a latter-day Marxism, to be sure, that prevails in the developing countries today. Marx's original concepts of a polarization in an advanced capitalist society between industrial proletariat and bourgeoisie are squeezed into various straitjackets in order to fit societies actually based on semi-feudal agriculture, primitive handicrafts, and an almighty bureaucracy or military clique. The real attraction of Marxism-Leninism, however distorted, consists (especially for the intellectual group, such as there is) in the simplified, easy-to-understand scheme of society and in the ready availability of villains to explain the abysmal social evils of these societies.

168

The most popular among these villains is imperialism. The specific connotation of this concept in the modernizing nations of our period far exceeds the original meaning of empire policy or of territorial expansion. It also exceeds its later interpretation as a necessary outlet for the surplus product or capital of the industrialized capitalist countries. Imperialism, as seen today in Latin America, in particular, means for groups committed to communism any policy or action of a Western nation that is at odds with the foreign policy aims of the Soviet Union. The expansionist policies of the latter are not associated with imperialism. Among noncommunist groups, imperialism is seen as closely linked to the old colonialism or as its latter-day successor. It is precisely this link, along with the recollection of colonial oppression, which explains to a large degree the attractiveness to these nations of an explanation of social evils in neo-Marxist-Leninist terms.

An essential element of this ideology consists of the association of foreign investment with imperialism. Even countries and regimes which have tried hard to attract foreign capital, especially for development-related projects, come to consider it imperialist once it has been in the country for a while. It is not intended here to exonerate foreign investors, particularly the large corporations which only too often bought favors from politicians and governments, destroyed communities and social institutions, or violated through lack of interest and understanding deeply rooted values and ways of life. But they also opened up resources which might otherwise have remained dormant for an indefinite period, and they contributed substantially to the supply of foreign exchange, tax revenues and jobs in some of these countries. At any rate, the desire for nationalization or outright confiscation of the assets of these foreign investors mixes with the Marxist belief that public ownership of the means of production is inevitable. The emphasis in modernizing countries is usually — not entirely in the Marxist vein — on the nationalization of basic resources, such as minerals and soil, which are seen as the irreplaceable heritage of the nation that should not be allowed to be in alien hands, even if without their action, the very existence of these resources might have remained unknown.

It is at this point that the originally internationalist Marxism blends hazily with what used to be its very opposite: nationalism. This is achieved through the concept of "economic dependence" which some modernizing nations, or groups within them, make responsible for the lag in national development. The dependence concept is often vague. It may range from a high share of exports and/or imports in the national product (which, of course, is also true of many industrialized countries) to the role of foreign investment in the national economy, the use of foreign sources in public or private financing, or foreign ownership of transportation facilities. Nationalization thus assumes a double meaning: in one sense it refers to the transfer of resources and productive facilities to nationals of the country concerned, while in the other, Marxist sense it means a transition to public ownership, regardless of whether foreign or national property is involved.

In any case, the revolution aimed at is partly of a nationalist and partly of a Marxian character. A decisive aspect of the revolutionary change refers to a process through which the nation is to take development into its own hands. This indeed presupposes the existence of an effective public administration and of political institutions equipped to supervise it. Widespread experience has shown that this tends to be the principal bottleneck of national modernization no matter what may have been the sins of foreign imperialists. Development planning and its non-inflationary implementation, in particular, require a kind of public administration which is far more difficult to achieve than revolutionary phraseology assumes. In order to promise success, such planning requires an integration of economic, social and political institutions, organization of human resources and community participation, urbanization and rural development, welfare services and social mobility, and quite a few other policies, with an effective machinery of implementation. The chief administrative obstacle tends to be not mere lack of training, though this too is important, but the frequent absence of a suitable *motivation* for national modernization and progress that plagues administration and politics in most developing countries. Many students of the problem in these countries hope to overcome this lack through an association of development with socialist motivation.

Development and Socialism

In its simplest form this association refers to the spirit of community feelings and cooperation which is so badly needed in order to make development effective. On a somewhat more sophisticated level, the connection is established by the need for an affirmative work motivation and strong feelings of responsibility for a productive performance on the part of the workers and other economic groups, and by a general realization of the psychological — not only economic and technological — problems that are implicit in development. Modernization in other words, is felt by many to require a socialist motivation based on a corresponding institutional framework.

From a somewhat different angle, the example of the Soviet Union transforming itself in one generation from a backward, war-torn peasant country into the second industrial power in the world has impressed more than a few modernizing nations in our period; and the Soviet Union and other communist regimes, for reasons we need not go into here, persist in calling themselves socialist thus contributing to the semantic and conceptual confusion surrounding the international debate about socio-economic and political systems.

The genuine, substantive problem facing the newly modernizing nations in this respect is whether the feat of the Soviet Union in jumping over the earlier phases of economic development that were experienced in Western Europe, and going almost straight from agrarian feudalism to industrial collectivism can be duplicated elsewhere, especially in much smaller countries without even the limited industrial starting point that prerevolutionary Russia had. More generally, assumptions that there are any fixed stages of economic growth that each developing country has to pass through have aroused growing skepticism.

Socialism, it is true, is not everywhere associated with either the specific planning mechanism or the totalitarian regime of the Soviet Union. It is seen by many as a general set of socio-ethical principles and motivations which are neither capitalist nor communist. Yet, a certain attractiveness of the Soviet example to newly modernizing countries has resulted from two of its major aspects: first, the necessity of a planning process designed to stimulate and channel economic and social change, even allowing for the fact that development plans have only too often remained on the level of a mere Declaration of Intention without an effective mechanism of implementation; and, second, the lure of totalitarianism as a seemingly effective if not indispensable tool of fast and sweeping development. It is only too often overlooked that totalitarian regimes with their lack of public control or criticism tend to be quite inefficient and often corrupt, though they are very good at concealing such evils over a long period; and that a totalitarian regime, once installed, is extremely difficult to get rid of

171

even when the overwhelming majority of the population would want to do so. At any rate, any association of socialism or planning with totalitarianism is artificial and by no means inevitable, but it is fairly widespread in modernizing areas.

Economic Development or Socio-Cultural Transformation?

An even more crucial question is increasingly being raised in the developing countries with reference to the true content of a meaningful development. It was mentioned earlier that fewer nations and groups are now satisfied with another percent or two of annual economic growth, or with continuing emulation of the wealthier nations, including their individual consumption habits. The Pearson Report, it is true, found that despite the great diversity of development needs "a common purpose emerges in nearly every country: to reduce poverty; to ensure minimum levels of education, health, housing and food to every citizen; to increase control over nature by the nation and the individual; to broaden the opportunity for choice." [2] However, awareness has been growing of the uniqueness of each national or cultural group and of its specific needs. There is also a growing recognition of the extent of the changes in values and attitudes that are required to bring about those patterns of work, production, and productivity that *are* recognized as valid and necessary in the interest of accepted social aims.

A further question then suggests itself about the extent to which the population concerned or its leadership groups consider such transformation of values and attitudes desirable; is it worth the price, from their point of view, especially if a prolonged *anomie* should threaten in such a case? Some will answer that progress in health, education, and income is well worth it. Others, for a variety of reasons which may be either of the conservative or the revolutionary kind, may reject any lasting removal of the old value system or else regard such removal as impossible through any conscious public action, most of all through any foreign aid.

At any rate, development now appears as a far more complex, comprehensive, and time-consuming process than the apostles of international imitation, technological adaptation, and rapid economic growth assumed only yesterday. To this comes the increasing recognition both in the poor and the wealthy countries of the impact of irrational factors (however defined specifically) within

172

social life in general and the development process in particular. What appeared in the past to some or all of the nations of North America and Western Europe as rational, and therefore as the inevitable future of people in every other area and phase of development as well, has now begun to look quite irrational or, at least, inapplicable to many developing populations in Asia, Africa and Latin America. To restate the point, they no longer feel guilty and inferior if they have accepted from West only some technological and organizational methods but not its values or interpretations of the meaning of life.

Unfortunately, they have been quick in accepting some of the irrational experiences from the West and applying them to their own urge for development — especially the mentality and methods of totalitarianism. In more than one case this mentality is closely related to age-old cultural patterns and social structures, so that the dubious modernization by such methods comes easily and almost naturally. This is especially true of trends in various newly independent or newly formed nations of Africa. The rationalization of totalitarianism is then supplied by the claim — sometimes readily accepted by development specialists from advanced countries — that there cannot be any modernization of a speedy and efficient nature in new, small and poorly integrated nations unless they are ruled by a firm hand, usually meaning a totalitarian dictator.

There is not a trace of evidence that this is actually required and much evidence to the contrary, as the recent case of Uganda shows. A totalitarian regime, which is essentially arbitrary rule based on demagogy rather than genuine participation of the rank and file, tends to be (or to become) a serious impediment to development, not a requirement for it. In extreme cases, dictated chauvinism may lead to a refusal to develop, not only by attempted withdrawal from the world scene (as in the case of Burma) but by indiscriminate elimination of all the Western influences that have already penetrated into the life of the population. This new version of The Myth of the Happy Savage is as unrealistic as the older one. Totalitarianism, be it in the West or the East, leads to savage myths and practices but nobody has shown yet that it is even an acceptable path to development.

Can Development be Aided?

The preceding discussion raises serious questions about the

extent to which development can be aided from the outside. For the imitative approach, this question did not exist: *of course* the developed nations, being wealthier in terms of per capita income, were also more advanced, *of course* the future of the less fortunate nations consisted in trying to emulate them, and *of course* the advanced ones had the facilities and perhaps the moral duty to help their poorer brethren to rise to their own supposed state of near perfection. Thus a huge international network of development aids was built up to cope with the economic, financial, technological, administrative, political, psychological, and educational aspects of development. Humanitarian measures and emergency aids, technical assistance, infrastructure, capital supply, all blended in a huge establishment of aid activities which were rarely integrated with the scattered national efforts into a clear-cut development policy and were even more rarely seen as a *two-way* or multilateral flow of experiences and intellectual resources.

The agencies trying to help ranged from national aid offices of the United States, Great Britain, France, Western Germany, Japan, Switzerland, and others to the Soviet block including COMECON. To these were added the United Nations Development Program (UNDP), UNESCO, FAO, ILO, WHO, UNIDO, the World Food Program, the World Bank with IFC and IDA, UNCTAD, IMF, GATT, OECD, the regional development banks for Latin America, the Caribbean, Asia and Africa, the Colombo Plan, the Organization of American States, international commodity agreements, and the activities of various federations of cooperatives, trade unions and churches. The list could be expanded.

It is not intended to minimize these often admirable efforts on the international level or the results they have yielded in specific cases. Yet, the net result of all these efforts is very limited. Worse than that, both the aid givers and the recipients wonder whether they have not been barking up the wrong tree and whether there is a substitute for, or an important supplement to, an essentially home-grown development effort supported by the bulk of the population through active participation. Without such a setting, aid givers will often see the tasks to be met quite differently from the recipients, and the latter will sooner or later tend to overcompensate for their inferiority feelings toward the wealthy but insensitive benefactors. Mutual mistrust will result, most of all in the many cases in which racial differences are involved.

What then is the solution? There is not any one patent formula. Simple withdrawal of the wealthy nations would likewise solve nothing. Limitation of aid to cases of a spontaneous, specific and

174

publicly supported request over a well-defined period would be far more promising, especially if future channels are to be increasingly multilateral or international. Most of all, everybody concerned needs to be aware of the almost limitless variety of the processes of socio-economic and cultural change, which have thus far been summed up conveniently, if vaguely and often unrealistically, under the broad concept of development.

Notes

Notes to Chapter 1

1. Henry G. Aubrey, *Coexistence: Economic Challenge and Response* (Washington, National Planning Association, 1961), p. 265.

Notes to Chapter 2

1. For a schematic presentation of the relationships discussed in this and the preceding sections, see the Appendix to this chapter.
2. For a comparative approach, see Maurice F. Neufeld, *Poor Countries and Authoritarian Rule* (Ithaca, N.Y., Cornell, 1965). Also, K.H. Silvert, ed., *Expectant Peoples: Nationalism and Development* (New York, Random House, 1963).
3. Somewhat related is Haya de la Torre's famous concept of Indoamerica and his interpretation of "Indoamerican Unity as Popular Conscience," Víctor Raúl Haya de la Torre, *Pensamiento Político*, vol. 1 (Lima, 1961); also "El Plan de Acción," speech of March 5, 1961, in vol. 4. On APRA and other populist movements in Latin America, Victor Alba, *Historia del Movimiento Obrero en América* (Mexico, 1964), esp. Ch. VII. On the relations between populism and Marxism, the papers by Aníbal Pinto and T.S. Di Tella in Claudio Véliz, ed., *Obstacles to Change in Latin America* (London, 1965). Populism as such is not, however, an especially useful category for the purposes of this discussion.
4. Fidel Castro, "I Am a Marxist-Leninist," reprinted in translation in Paul E. Sigmund, ed., *The Ideologies of the Developing Nations* (New York, Praeger, 1963), pp. 270 ff.
5. Léopold Sédar Senghor, *On African Socialism* (New York, American Society of African Culture, 1964). Haya de la Torre, see footnote 3. Also, C.F. Andrain, "Democracy and Socialism: Ideologies of African Leaders," in David E. Apter, ed., *Ideology and Discontent* (New York, 1964);

Elliot J. Berg, "Socialism and Economic Development in Tropical Africa," *Quarterly Journal of Economics*, vol. LXXVIII, Nov. 1964; Willard A. Belling, ed., *The Role of Labor in African Nation-Building* (New York, 1967).

6. Anthony Leeds, "Brazil and the Myth of Francisco Juliāc," in Joseph Maier and Richard W. Weatherhead, eds., *Politics of Change in Latin America* (New York, Praeger, 1964), ch. 10.

7. For international comparisons, Walter Galenson, ed., *Labor and Economic Development* (New York, Wiley, 1959), and *Labor in Developing Economies* (Berkeley, Univ. of Calif., 1962). Also, Adolf Sturmthal, "Some Thoughts on Labor and Political Action," *University of Illinois Bulletin*, January 1963.

8. Albert Lauterbach, *Enterprise in Latin America: Business Attitudes in a Developing Economy* (Ithaca, N.Y., Cornell, 1966), esp. ch. 1. See also ch. 5 of the present book.

9. Compare the books by Robert J. Alexander, *Organized Labor in Latin America* (New York, Free Press, 1965), and *Latin American Politics and Government* (New York, Harper, 1965), esp. ch. XI, on "The Union's Nation-Building Role." Also Bruce H. Millen, *The Political Role of Labor in Developing Countries* (Washington, Brookings, 1963), esp. pp. 73ff.

10. For an interesting statement on related problems, Singapore National Trade Unions Congress, "The Role of Trade Unions in Securing Social Change," *ICFTU Economic and Social Bulletin*, Brussels, XIV/I, January 1966.

11. Fred R. van der Mehden, *Politics of the Developing Nations* (New York, 1964), ch. VI. For a socio-political interpretation of Latin American militarism, Victor Alba, *El Militarismo: Ensayo sobre un fenómeno político-social Iberoamericano* (Mexico, 1959).

12. Compare James L. Payne, *Labor and Politics in Peru* (New Haven, 1965), especially on the conditions under which violence has been considered part of a normal pattern of social relations.

13. For a somewhat different viewpoint, Manfred Halpern, "The Revolution of Modernization in National and International Society," in Carl J. Friedrich, ed., *Revolution* (New York, 1966).

Notes to Chapter 3

1. For example, Henry S. Commager, *The American Mind* (New Haven, Yale, 1962).

2. "The central element of the American metaphysic is the belief that American institutions are more 'natural' and therefore better than those of other people." Max Lerner, *America as a Civilization* (New York, 1957), Simon & Schuster, p. 920. "The belief that Americanism can be more or less complete, and that this relative completeness is above all a matter of will, is the most important component in the attitude of most Americans toward the inhabitants of the rest of the world." Geoffrey Gorer, *The American People* (New York, Cresset Press, 1948), p. 220.

3. "And, just because our emotional need for security is so great, we tend to impute the utmost permanence to our assumptions." Robert S. Lynd, *Knowledge for What?* (Princeton, Univ. Press, 1948), p. 58.

4. Erik H. Erikson, *Childhood and Society* (New York, Norton, 1950), p. 246.

5. Compare Martha Weinman Lear, *The Child Worshipers* (New York, 1963). "The parent who is too yielding gives the child nothing to come up against — No child can test out his developing strength by swimming in treacle." Anthony Storr, *Human Aggression* (New York, 1968), p. 45.

6. On the intricacies of the formation of time concepts in children, see the writings of Jean Piaget, eg. *The Construction of Reality in the Child* (New York, 1954), ch. IV.

7. Norman Mailer, *The Naked and the Dead* (New York, Rinehart, 1948), p. 704.

8. Compare Erikson, *Childhood and Society*, ch. 8.

9. John Dollard, *Frustration and Aggression* (New Haven, Yale, 1939), p. 156.

10. Richard Hofstadter, *The Paranoid Style in American Politics* (New York, Knopf, 1965).

11. In the judgment of Lord Bryce, in the late nineteenth century, the American voter "is like a sailor who knows the spars and ropes of the ship and is expert at working her, but is ignorant of geography and navigation; who can perceive that some of the officers are smart and others dull, but cannot judge which of them is qualified to use the sextant or will best keep his head during a hurricane." James Bryce, "The American Character in the 1880's," in Michael McGiffert, ed., *The Character of Americans* (Chicago, 1964), p. 69.

12. David Kraslow and Stuart H. Loory, *The Secret Search for Peace in Vietnam* (New York, 1968). Also, J. William Fulbright, *The Arrogance of Power* (New York, Vintage, 1966). On the concepts of "defensive imperialism" and "patronizing imperialism," Roberto de Oliveira Campos, *Reflections on Latin American Development* (Austin, Texas, Univ. of Texas, 1967), chapter on "United States—Latin American Relations."

13. Compare Edward McNall Burns, *The American Idea of Mission: Concepts of National Purpose and Destiny* (New Brunswick, N.J., Rutgers Univ., 1957). "Power tends to confuse itself with virtue," Fulbright, *Arrogance of Power* p. 3.

14. Compare Albert K. Weinberg, *Manifest Destiny: A Study of Nationalist Expansionism in American History* (Gloucester, Mass., 1958), esp. ch. 14: "International Police Power." Also: "The missionary instinct in foreign affairs may, in a curious way, reflect a deficiency rather than an excess of national self-confidence." Fulbright, *Arrogance of Power*, p. 21. "We are a frightening people because the atrocities we commit hardly touch our official self-righteousness, our invincible conviction of our moral infallibility...the zeal with which we have pursued an irrational war suggests the internal impulses of hatred and violence demanding outlet and shaping our foreign policy to their ends." Arthur M. Schlesinger, Jr., "America 1968: The Politics of Violence," *Harper's*, August 1968, pp. 19ff.

15. "It is my opinion that one reason for American distress is the American belief in American invulnerability and American omnipotence... Many,

178

Lauterbach's generalized or global approaches contrast with the specific case studies in crises found in Robert E. Scott's <u>Latin American Modernization Problems</u> or Stanley David and Lousi Goodman's readings, <u>Workers and Managers in Latin America</u> or F. LaMond Tullis, <u>Politics and Social Change in Third World Countries.</u>

very many Americans, it seems to me, find it inconceivable that an American policy, announced and carried out by the American government, acting with the support of the American people, does not immediately succeed. If it does not, this, they feel, must be because of stupidity or treason." D.W. Brogan, *American Aspects* (New York, Harper, 1964), pp. 11, 17.

16. Campos, *Latin American Development*, pp. 132 and 158. See also Edward Stillman, "The End of American Innocence, " *Yale Review*, autumn 1968.
17. "Religious piety is as much a part of American politics as campaign buttons and bumper stickers." Edward B. Fiske, "There's Piety in Our Politics," *New York Times*, January 15, 1967.
18. "Men sacrifice for a religious opinion their friends, their family, and their country; one can consider them devoted to the pursuit of intellectual goals which they came to purchase at so high a price. One sees them, however, seeking with almost equal eagerness material wealth and moral satisfaction; heaven in the world beyond, and well-being and liberty in this one." Alexis de Tocqueville, *Democracy in America* (New York, Vintage Books, 1954), vol. I, p. 45. From a different angle, James A. Knight, M.D., *For the Love of Money* (Philadelphia, 1968).
19. "It is precisely in this matter of trying to live by contrasting rules of the game that one of the most characteristic aspects of our American culture is to be seen." Lynd, *Knowledge for What?* p. 59.
20. John C. Flugel, *Man, Morals, and Society* (New York, International Universities Press, 1945).
21. Hans J. Morgenthau, "A Question of Choices," *ADA World Magazine*, Washington, Americans for Democratic Action, vol. 1, nr. 6, March 1966, p. 2M.

Notes to Chapter 4

1. Albert Lauterbach, *Man, Motives and Money*, 2nd ed. (Ithaca: Cornell University Press, 1959), chapter 3.
2. For a summary of the results of this research, see Albert Lauterbach, "Managerial Attitudes in Western Europe," *American Economic Review*, 45 (2), May 1955, 675ff.; and "Perceptions of Management," *Administrative Science Quarterly*, June 1957.
3. G.L.S. Shackle, *Expectation in Economics* (Cambridge, Univ. Press, 1949), p. 127.
4. See, for example, F.H. Harbison and E.W. Burgess, "Modern Management in Western Europe," *American Journal of Sociology*, 60 (1954), 15-23.
5. Abram Kardiner, *The Psychological Frontiers of Society*, (New York, Columbia Univ., 1945), pp. 420-22.
6. Werner Sombart, "Die Abneigung gegen die Klarlegung der Markt- und Konjunkturverhaeltnisse," *Der Moderne Kapitalismus*, vol. 2, pt. 1 (Munich-Leipzig, Duncker & Humblot, 1921), pp. 60f.
7. Erich Fromm, *Escape from Freedom* (New York, Rinehart, 1941), chapter 2.

179

8. J.A. Schumpeter, "The Instability of Capitalism," *Economic Journal*, Vol. 38 (1928), reprinted in his *Essays* (Cambridge, Mass.: Addison-Wesley Publishing Co., 1951). See also his *Capitalism, Socialism, and Democracy*, 3rd ed. (New York: Harper and Brothers, 1950), pt. 2.

9. Howard Bowen, *Social Responsibilities of the Businessman* (New York, Harper, 1953). "The Moral History of U.S. Business," *Fortune*, December 1949.

10. B.R. Fisher and S.B. Withey, *Big Business As the People See It*, University of Michigan, Survey Research Center, 1951, especially pp. xi and 172.

11. C. Wright Mills, *White Collar* (New York, Oxford Univ. Press, 1953), pp. 239ff. Compare Neil W. Chamberlain, *Union Challenge to Management Control* (New York, Harper, 1948); also Clark Kerr and Abraham Siegel, "The Structuring of the Labor Force in Industrial Society," *Industrial and Labor Relations Review*, 8 (1955), 151-168.

12. Oswald W. Knauth, *Managerial Enterprise* (New York, Norton, 1948), pp. 180f.

13. Robert E. Lane, *The Regulation of Businessmen: Social Conditions of Government Economic Control* (New Haven, Yale, 1954), pp. 19f., 31f.

14. Forest D. Siefkin, "Executive Decisions at the Top Level," *American Economic Review*, 41 (2), May 1951, pp. 91f.

15. Thomas H. Sanders, *Effects of Taxation on Executives* (Boston, Harvard Univ., 1951); Lewis H. Kimmel, *Taxes and Economic Incentives* (Washington, D.C., Brookings, 1950).

16. G.W.F. Hallgarten, "Adolf Hitler and German Heavy Industry," *Journal of Economic History*, 12 (1952), 222-246. Arthur Schweitzer, *Big Business in the Third Reich* (Bloomington, Ind., Indiana Univ. 1964). Also Gerard Braunthal, *The Federation of German Industry in Politics* (Ithaca, N.Y., Cornell Univ. 1965), part one.

17. University of Michigan, Survey Research Center, "People's Attitudes toward Inflation and Spending," mimeo. Cf. George Katona and Eva Mueller, *Consumer Attitudes and Demand, 1950-52* (Ann Arbor, 1953), chapter 4, and *Consumer Expectations 1953-56* (Ann Arbor, 1957), chapter 7.

18. George Katona, *Psychological Analysis of Economic Behavior* New York, McGraw-Hill, 1951), p. 249.

19. Melvin T. Copeland, *The Executive at Work* (Cambridge, Mass., 1951), p. 117.

20. Sombart, "Das Wirtschaftsleben im Zeitalter des Hochkapitalismus," *Der Moderne Kapitalismus*,Vol. 3, pt. 2 (Munich-Leipzig, 1927), chapter 43; Frank H. Knight, *Risk, Uncertainty, and Profit* (Boston, Houghton-Mifflin, 1921), pp. 47, 247ff.

21. John K. Galbraith, *American Capitalism* (Boston, Houghton-Mifflin, 1952), chapter 6. Cf., for a psychoanalytic view, Paul Federn, "Mental Factors in the World Depression," *Journal of Nervous and Mental Diseases*, vol. 79 (1934).

Notes to Chapter 5

1. For more specific research data on that area, see Lauterbach, *Enterprise*

in Latin America: Business Attitudes in a Developing Economy (Ithaca, N.Y., Cornell Univ., 1966).

2. Compare Heinz Hartmann, "Managers and Entrepreneurs: A Useful Distinction?" in *Administrative Science Quarterly*, March 1959.
3. See Albert Lauterbach, *Man, Motives, and Money*, 2nd ed. (Ithaca, New York, Cornell, 1959), chapters 1 and 2. Also, James K. Dent, "Organizational Correlates of the Goals of Business Managements," *Journal of Personnel Psychology* vol. 12, no. 3, Autumn 1959. Albert Lauterbach, *Managerial Attitudes in Chile* (Instituto de Economía, Universidad de Chile, Santiago, 1960).
4. Compare Fritz Redlich, "Business Leadership: Diverse Origins and Variant Forms," *Economic Development and Cultural Change*, Vol. vi, no. 3, April 1958. Another school of thought, however (see Note 8) assumes that industrial growth has its intrinsic logic of managerial development and that management can be defined anywhere in terms of an economic resource, a system of authority, and a class or elite.
5. United Nations, *Management of Industrial Enterprises in Under-Developed Countries* (New York, 1958), p. 5.
6. United Nations, *Management of Industrial Enterprises*, p. 24. See also, C.R.Wynne-Roberts, "Labour Aspects of Management," *Industrialization and Productivity*, Bulletin No. 2, United Nations, March 1959.
7. G. Robson, "Use of Accounting as an Aid to Management in Industrial Enterprises in Underdeveloped Countries," *Industrialization and Productivity*, Bulletin No. 1, United Nations, April 1958.
8. Clark Kerr, John T. Dunlop, Frederick H. Harbison, and Charles A. Myers, *Industrialism and Industrial Man* (Cambridge, Mass, Harvard Univ., 1960), p. 7.
9. For a case study of a culture clash in foreign investment, see K.H. Silvert, "A Matter of Business," in *American Universities Field Staff*, Argentina series, April 20, 1958. Compare R.M. Powell, "Latin American Perception of U.S. Capitalism," in *Business Horizons*, vol 2, no. 4, Winter 1959. From a different angle, W.F. Whyte, and A.R. Holmberg, "Human Problems of U.S. Enterprise in Latin America," *Human Organization*, Fall 1956.
10. On the employment aspect of industrialization, see International Labour Office, *Fiscal Measures for Employment Promotion in Developing Countries* (Geneva 1972)

Notes to Chapter 6

1. This chapter was written in collaboration with the psychiatrist Joseph Wilder, M.D.
2. Erich Fromm, *Escape from Freedom* (New York, Rinehart, 1941), p. 11.
3. J. Eaton and R. Weil, *Culture and Mental Disorders* (Glencoe, Illinois, Free Press, 1956).
4. Sigmund Freud, *Das Unbehagen in der Kultur* (Vienna, Internationaler Psychoanalytischer Verlag, 1930).
5. Marvin K. Opler, *Culture, Psychiatry, and Human Values* (Springfield, Ill.,

Thomas, 1954). See also, Lawrence K. Frank, *Society as the Patient* (New Brunswick, Rutgers Univ., 1948).

6. James L. Halliday, *Psychosocial Medicine* (New York, Norton, 1948).
7. Erich Fromm, *The Sane Society* (New York, Rinehart, 1955), pp. 67, 73, 76.
8. Joseph Wortis, *Soviet Psychiatry* (Baltimore, Williams & Wilkins, 1950). V. Guilarovsky, "The Contemporary Situation in Soviet Psychotherapy," in *Progress in Psychotherapy*, VI. III, J.H.Masserman and J.L. Moreno, eds. (New York, Grune & Stratton, 1958). Raymond A. Bauer, *The New Man in Soviet Psychology* (Cambridge, Mass., Harvard Univ., 1952).
9. J. Bowlby, *Maternal Care and Mental Health* (Geneva: World Health Organization, 1952).
10. Milbank Memorial Fund, *The Family Health Maintenance Demonstration* (New York, 1954). O. Speck, *Kinder Erwerbstaetiger Muetter* (Stuttgart, Enke, 1956).
11. World Federation for Mental Health, *Mental Health and Infant Development*, K. Soddy, ed. (London, Routledge, 1955).
12. B. Pasamanick, H. Knobloch, and A.M. Lilienfeld, "Socioeconomic Status and Some Precursors of Neuropsychiatric Disorder," *American Journal of Orthopsychiatry*, 26: 594, 1956. Ch. de Lauve, "Milieu Social et Psychiatrie Infantile," *Revue de Neuropsychiatrie Infantile*, 4: 5-6, 1956. N.W. Ackerman and M.L. Behrens, "The Family Group and Family Therapy," in *Progress in Psychotherapy*, Vol. III.
13. Eli Ginzberg, et al., *Occupational Choice* (New York, Columbia Univ., 1951). Eli Ginzberg, et al., *Psychiatry and Military Manpower Policy* (New York, Columbia Univ., 1953). International Labour Office, *Human Resources for Industrial Development* (Geneva, 1967), and *The World Employment Programme* (Geneva, 1969).
14. Freud, *Das Unbehagen*, p. 31.
15. J.W. Bick, Jr., "Occupational neuroses," *Diseases of the Nervous System*, 16:1, 1955.
16. Odegaard: "The Incidence of Psychoses in Various Occupations," *International Journal of Social Psychiatry*, 2: 2, 1956. R.E. Clark, "Psychoses, Income, and Occupational Prestige," in R. Bendix and S.M. Lipset, eds., *Class, Status and Power* (Glencoe, Illinois, Free Press, 1953).
17. R.M.Frumkin, and M.Z. Frumkin, "Environment and mental illness," *Ohio State Medical Journal*, 52: 32, 1956.
18. R.E.L. Faris and H.W. Dunham, *Mental Disorders in Urban Areas* (Chicago, Univ. of Chicago Press, 1939).
19. H. Goldhamer and A. Marshall, *Psychosis and Civilization* (Glencoe, Ill., Free Press, 1953). S. Kirson Weinberg, *Society and Personality Disorders* (New York, Prentice, 1953). Arnold M. Rose, ed., *Mental Health and Mental Disorder: A Sociological Approach* (New York, Norton, 1955). W.A. Scott, "Social Psychological Correlates of Mental Health," *Psychological Bulletin* 55: 2, 1958.
20. A.B. Hollingshead and F.C. Redlich, *Social Class and Mental Illness: A Community Study* (New York, Wiley, 1958).
21. Paul M. Roman and Harrison M. Trice, *Schizophrenia and the Poor* (Ithaca, New York, 1967), Cornell Univ. pp. 64f.
22. C. Kluckhohn and H.A. Murray, eds., *Personality in Nature, Society, and Culture*, 2nd ed. (New York, Knopf, 1956), p. 129.

23. A.H. Leighton; J.A. Clausen, and R.N. Wilson, eds., *Explorations in Social Psychiatry* (New York, Basic Books, 1957).
24. G. Schmoelders, "Die psychischen Grundlagen des Eigentum- und Geld-verhaltens," mimeo. (Cologne, 1957), and *Psychologie des Geldes* (Hamburg, Rowohlt, 1966). Also, his *Finanz- und Steuerpsychologie* (Hamburg, Rowohlt, 1970).
25. John Dollard, *Caste and Class in a Southern Town*, 2nd ed. (New York, Harper, 1949); *idem* and L. Ovesey, *The Mark of Oppression: A Psychological Study of the American Negro* (New York, Norton, 1951).
26. H.A. Storrow, "Psychiatric Treatment and the Lower-Class Neurotic," *Archives of General Psychiatry*, 6: 469, 1962. M.A. Greenblatt and M.R. Sharaf, "Poverty and Mental Health," *Psychiatric Opinion*, vol. 5/3, August 1968.
27. A.F. Henry and J.G. Short, *Suicide and Homicide: Some Economic, Sociological and Psychological Aspects of Aggression* (Glencoe, Free Press, 1954).
28. Milbank Memorial Fund, *Epidemiology of Mental Disorder* (New York, 1950), p. 56.
29. Joseph Wilder, "Beyond Parents: Parents as a Socioeconomic Phenomenon," in Stanley Lesse, ed., *An Evaluation of the Results of the Psychotherapies* (Springfield, Ill., 1968).
30. Karen Horney, *The Neurotic Personality of our Time* (New York, Norton, 1937), p. 188.
31. R.W. and M. Conwell, and M.B. Arrill, "An Approach to Measuring the Cost of Mental Illness," *American Journal of Psychiatry*, 124: 6, December 1967. This does not allow fully for manifold *indirect* costs of the widespread nonrational behavior in economic situations.
32. Mike Gorman, *Every Other Bed* (Cleveland, World Publishing Co., 1956). M. Greenblatt and D. Levinson, eds., *The Patient and the Mental Hospital* (Glencoe, Ill., Free Press, 1956).
33. B.M. Spinley, *The Deprived and the Privileged: Personality Development in English Society* (London, Routledge, 1953), p. 129. R.K. Merton, "Social Psychology of Housing," *Current Trends in Social Psychology* (Pittsburgh, Univ. of Pittsburgh, 1948).
34. Margaret Mead, ed., *Cultural Patterns and Technical Change* (New York, Mentor, 1955).

Notes to Chapter 7

1. Albert Lauterbach, *Enterprise in Latin America* (Ithaca, N.Y., Cornell Univ., 1966).
2. Compare Hirschman's "Principle of the Hiding Hand." "...far from seeking out and taking up challenges, people typically take on and plunge into new tasks because of the erroneously presumed *absence* of a challenge, because the task looks easier and more manageable than it will turn out to be." Albert O.Hirschman, *Development Projects Observed* (Washington, Brookings, 1967), p. 13.
3. Compare Theodore Geiger, *The Conflicted Relationship; The West and*

the Transformation of Asia, Africa, and Latin America (New York, 1967). Also, Evsey D. Domar, "Reflections on Economic Development," *The American Economist*, vl. X/l, spring 1966. Related problems are discussed in various writings of Gunnar Myrdal, most recently in *Asian Drama* (New York, Pantheon, 1968), esp. vol. I, prologue, and vol. III, appendix 2.

4. Kurt Martin and John Knapp, eds., *The Teaching of Development Economics: Its Position in the Present State of Knowledge* (Chicago, 1967).
5. For a divergent, neo-behaviorist point of view, John H. Kunkel, "Values and Behavior in Economic Development," *Economic Development and Cultural Change*, vol. XIII/3, April 1965.
6. Association for Comparative Economics, "Convergence and Divergence of Economic Systems in the Process of Socioeconomic Development," Report of International Conference in Bellagio, Italy, September 3—9, 1967, mimeographed (Northern Illinois University, DeKalb, Illinois), especially statements by K.W. Kapp and Arthur Schweitzer.
7. One school of thought, conversely, attempts "to explain those aspects of the process of development that are quantitatively similar for all countries" and believes that "the process of development is a problem of adopting various alternative means to achieve a common statistical end." Robert F. Dernberger, "Economic Development: A Problem in Comparative Economic Systems?" Association for Comparative Economics, "Economic Systems and Underdevelopment" Report of Miami Beach Conference, Nov. 11-13, 1965 (mimeographed).
8. Compare Arthur Schweitzer, "Economic Systems and Economic History," *Journal of Economic History*, XXV/4, December 1965.
9. Koefod defines economic system as "a set of culturally consistent structural, organizational, legal, institutional and other relevant variables." Paul E. Koefod, "Some General Problems of Economic Development," *Land Economics*, vol. XLII/3, August 1966.
10. Albert Lauterbach, *Kapitalismus und Sozialismus in neuer Sicht* (Hamburg, Rowohlt, 1963).
11. Gunnar Adler-Karlsson, "Functional Socialism: A Concept for the Analysis of Convergence of National Economies," Paper for the Third European Peace Research Society Conference, Vienna 1966 (mimeographed).
12. Joseph A. Schumpeter, *The Theory of Economic Development* (Cambridge, Mass., Addison-Wesley, 1955); *Capitalism, Socialism and Democracy*, 3rd ed. (New York, Harper, 1950).
13. Albert O. Hirschman, *The Strategy of Economic Development* (New Haven, Yale, 1958); also *Development Projects Observed* (Washington, Brookings, 1967).
14. See chapters 1 and 2.
15. This has been pointed out in various United Nations studies, such as *Planning for Economic Development* (New York, 1966), and *World Economic Survey 1966*, part I. See also Albert Waterston, *Development Planning* (Baltimore, John Hopkins Press, 1965).
16. K.W. Kapp, "Social Costs in Economic Development," in G.P. Sicat and Others, eds., *Economics and Development* (Quezon City, Univ. of the Philippines, 1965), ch. 12.

Notes to Chapter 8

1. Dudley Seers, "The Meaning of Development," paper given at the 11th World Conference of the Society for International Development, New Delhi, November 1969; reprinted by the Agricultural Development Council, New York, 1970.
2. *Partners in Development*. Report of the Commission on International Development, chairman: Lester B. Pearson. (New York: Praeger, 1969), p. 233.

Index

187

PRI in Mexico and the
Congress Party in India —
dominant but minor
  party opposition permitted.

Power élite: Mexico's
    Inner Circle leaders
    from PRI, CTM, CONCAMIN,
  CONCANACO, CNC —

India's Congress Party leadership
    & Indira Gandhi &
    Ministers of state —